IS DISABILITY RIG

RIGHTS

REPRODUCTIVE RIGHTS REPR

ORKERS' RIG

IOLENCE

ENVIRONMENTAL JUSTIC

A RIGHT

HTS IMMIGR

TOGETHER WE RISE

TOGETHER WE RISE
WAS CONCEIVED BY:
CASSADY FENDLAY
SARAH SOPHIE FLICKER
CINDI LEIVE
PAOLA MENDOZA

DEY ST.
An Imprint of WILLIAM MORROW

TOGETHER WE RISE

BEHIND THE SCENES AT THE PROTEST HEARD AROUND THE WORLD

THE WOMEN'S MARCH ORGANIZERS AND CONDÉ NAST

At the Women's March
in Washington, D.C.,
January 21, 2017.

"I AM NOT FREE WHILE ANY WOMAN IS UNFREE, EVEN WHEN HER SHACKLES ARE VERY DIFFERENT FROM MY OWN."

AUDRE LORDE, 1934–1992

"I LOVE NAPS BUT I STAY WOKE."

SIGN WORN BY A TODDLER AT THE WOMEN'S MARCH, OAKLAND, CALIFORNIA, JANUARY 21, 2017

DEDICATED TO WOMEN, DOCUMENTED AND UNDOCUMENTED: THE DAUGHTERS, THE MOTHERS, THE CAREGIVERS, THE WORKERS, THE TRANS WARRIORS, THE WITCHES, THE ARTISTS, THE REFUGEES, THE LEADERS. YOU ARE OUR LIGHT IN THE DARK.

The march as seen from the roof of the Voice of America offices on Independence Avenue in Washington, D.C.

CONTENTS

Washington, D.C.

PREFACE

Where were you on January 21, 2017? If you were like five million women from Washington, D.C., to Dar es Salaam to Seoul, you marched in towns large and small, on state capitols. You rode buses, took trains, carpooled with others, scraped together cash to pay the fare. You made signs, held your children in one hand and a sign in the other. You stood up to tyranny. You raised your voice.

You began to change the world.

The Women's Marches held around the globe that day constitute the single largest protest in world history. Let that sink in: *The single largest protest in world history.* As we write this, the march is still so recent that its ultimate impact has yet to be measured—will not be measured for decades—but already we can see the ripple effects, and they are seismic.

We are the national organizers of the Women's March—along with dozens of organizers, we planned and executed the Washington, D.C., protest, while around the world thousands of other organizers launched protests in their own communities, from 750,000 in Los Angeles to a one-person protest in Show Low, Arizona. And now we hope that the story of how the march was birthed will inspire you to continue to move forward during this moment of resistance.

Together We Rise is both the story of how it happened and the story of what will happen next, because the vision the organizers had for the march is also a vision of the future, when ours is a more equitable and inclusive country. Making change is hard work, and we want this book to be both road map and inspiration. And documenting history *matters*. So often women are erased from our history books. Not this time. Signs and T-shirts along the march route proclaimed "The Future Is Female," but so is the past—and unless women tell our own story, men of privilege will always rewrite history in their favor. We created this book so that no historian, pundit, or politician could claim what was ours. And what was yours.

We also want to shine a light on the woman-of-color-led resistance work that continues to be done across the country and that is so critical to our democracy and our humanity. When women lead, a different narrative emerges, one of collaboration—in which rather than being divided by race, sexual orientation, ability, or other factors, we are united, bringing all our identities to bear in favor of fundamental human equality.

What happens now, of course, is up to all of us. It was a march, but it was also only a first step. That's why we've included suggestions on how to take action on issues you care about (see page 297). And we're sharing the proceeds of this book with three grassroots, women-of-color-led nonprofits, The Gathering for Justice, SisterSong Women of Color Reproductive Justice Initiative, and Indigenous Women Rise. Your purchase of this book helps reform the criminal justice system, guarantees more women access to reproductive health, and uplifts indigenous women to organize for the betterment of their communities.

Together we marched on January 21. Together we march still. The moment is now. Together we rise.

BY JAMIA WILSON

INTRODUCTION

"You may shoot me with your words, you may cut me with your eyes, you may kill me with your hatefulness. But still, like air, I'll rise."

Poet, feminist, and racial justice advocate Maya Angelou wrote these words 40 years ago, long before a group of visionary women (many of whom had not yet been born) ignited the movement we now know as the resistance. The passion and determination of this small group brought Angelou's proclamation to life.

Rise, we did.

On January 21, 2017, five million women (and their allies) took to the streets around the world to stand up for their rights. This extraordinary moment had been made possible by an impassioned collective of organizers. In less than three months, they had done the unimaginable: Using activism as alchemy, they transformed one of the most divisive moments in American history—the election of Donald Trump—into an unprecedented movement that was both intergenerational and intersectional, embracing all aspects of its participants' identities. And the 653 marches in the United States and sister marches on all seven continents were only the beginning. A wave of protest and activism followed the march and sustained itself through the first year of the new administration.

In the days after the march, commentators mused on the scale and power of the crowds, the signs, the emotion. But the Women's March didn't "just happen." A team of organizers—including the four cochairs, Bob Bland, Tamika Mallory, Carmen Perez, and Linda Sarsour, plus Breanne Butler, Cassady Fendlay, Sarah Sophie Flicker, Janaye Ingram, Mia Ives-Rublee, Paola Mendoza, Ginny Suss, Vanessa Wruble, and many other devoted activists—worked long hours and encountered near-constant hurdles. They took cues from freedom fighters from the civil rights movement such as Angela Davis, Dolores Huerta, and Bernice King. They adopted strategies from other movements such as Black Lives Matter, the #NoDAPL movement, the DREAMer movement,

Jamia Wilson, a writer and activist, is the executive director and publisher of the Feminist Press.

the disability rights movement, and the anti–gun violence movement to set their own mega-movement into motion. And they worked with male allies like Harry Belafonte, Ted Jackson, and Michael Skolnik, while putting women—and specifically women of color—at the center of their leadership structure.

I am a woman of color. I was born in 1980 in Columbia, South Carolina, and grew up an expat in Saudi Arabia. I come from a long line of activists who "made a way out of no way," and that's why I heeded the call to show up on march day. The principles that guided the Women's March movement align deeply with my own family history of daring to resist and asserting one's humanity at all costs. My strong, black, feminist father marched in the 1970s to protest the incarceration of Joan Little, a cousin of his who came close to being executed by the state of North Carolina because she defended herself against sexual violence in a local jail after she was charged with breaking and entering. Growing up, I was fascinated by my mother's stories about her own involvement with the Student Nonviolent Coordinating Committee

ONE REASON TO PRESERVE THE HISTORY OF THE MARCH IS THAT ITS LESSONS CAN HELP US CONTINUE TO WORK FOR A BETTER FUTURE.

and the teach-ins she participated in. I learned from her that my grandfather was what they called a "race man," an NAACP member who traveled the South with his family, organizing meetings and marches to end segregation. It was my mother who persuaded me to march even though I was initially conflicted about participating—I felt betrayed by the 53 percent of white women who voted for Trump. Ultimately it was important to me to continue the involvement of our family line, and I was encouraged by Dr. Martin Luther King Jr.'s truth that "the arc of the moral universe is long, but it bends toward justice."

The story of the Women's March is a story of legacy and learning. One reason to bear witness, to preserve its history—as I have in my interviews with 30 people central to its creation and through the voices of others who attended and observed all over the world—is that the lessons in this document can help us continue to show up to work for a better future.

I'm an experienced organizer, but I engaged with the Women's March as both a participant and, frankly, a student. Over the weeks it was being planned, its social media and digital organizing, led by Alyssa Klein and Sophie Ellman-Golan, gave all of us a front-row seat to the step-by-step formation of a mass demonstration. Like millions of others, I watched, listened, and participated in spirited debates about inclusion, grieving the state of affairs and celebrating triumphs with the Women's March community through Instagram, Facebook Live, and Twitter chats. The living archive expanded day and night, building excitement, creating intrigue, and teaching us that something as simple as showing up is as beautifully messy as any other human endeavor—especially in the decentralized, fluid model the march organizers chose to follow. I may not have agreed with every decision that was made, but I supported the women who were making them and their courageous attempts at working together across differences to figure things out at breakneck speed—with backlash almost always guaranteed.

Over the years, I've attended more marches than I can count, but I knew this one was different when I encountered droves of pink-hatted women standing in line at fast-food restaurants and rest areas on the ride down from New York City to Washington, D.C. As I listened to Trump's swearing-in on the radio, my tension was eased by the sight of an endless stream of buses speeding by on the Beltway, decorated with signs calling for everything from labor rights to environmental justice.

On that unseasonably sunny Saturday morning in Washington, D.C., we came together under banners devoted to the protection and uplift of our communities and on behalf of voices that too often remain unheard. While I marched, I learned that back in New York the bells at St. Thomas Church on Fifth Avenue played "We Shall Overcome" as marchers passed its doors. I imagined my mother back in the sixties, lifting her voice in song alongside Dr. Martin Luther King Jr., Bayard Rustin, Ella Baker, and other marchers, and I wondered if she had felt the same flood of emotions back then that I was feeling that day in Washington. As I marched, I imagined telling my future children, "I was there! Not just for me, but for you, and for your grandchildren too." I knew I would be proud to say to them, "I was not silent. I was not complicit. We stood, together." And when my eyes met the gaze of an elderly white woman who was wearing a vintage yellow Jackie O–style suit, sitting in a wheelchair and holding a "Black Lives Matter" sign, I was reminded of the importance of radical solidarity being passed down from generation to generation.

The grim reality in our current world of the rise of authoritarianism and the emboldening of hate groups is chilling. Yet despite the terrain being the toughest that many of us have seen in our lifetime, we can look to our activist ancestors as a compass and a road map. And now we can also look to the march organizers, who, in the spirit of MLK before them, showed us that leadership is defined by being of service, seeking solutions, and working for the greater good. Together, the millions of souls who marched proved to the world that liberation comes not from a gilded tower, bombastic tweets, or a reality-TV empire, but instead from the energetic hope of true patriots (both documented and undocumented) who understand that we are all, as our sister marcher Gloria Steinem says, "linked, not ranked."

On January 21, the revolution was televised, tweeted, and live-streamed, but flashed by in what felt like a second. Although the march was one of the biggest mass demonstrations in recorded history, each of us experienced our own limited corner of the bigger picture, and the sum is so much more inspiring, insightful, and instructive than the parts we saw in our own individual cities and on our feeds—which is why a deep, behind-the-scenes look is critical to our understanding of what really happened.

It is too soon to know the full impact of the movement and of the Women's March organization, which is still forming its identity even as it continues to fight for equality, freedom of expression, and justice for all. This book, like the march itself, is only the beginning of a story. But we will feel the effects of millions of movement builders, artists, and

ON JANUARY 21, THE REVOLUTION WAS TELEVISED, TWEETED, AND LIVE-STREAMED, BUT FLASHED BY IN WHAT FELT LIKE A SECOND.

former armchair revolutionaries who showed up and marched to resist oppression and defend human rights, and we will see the impact of the record-breaking number of women now running for office for years to come. We can find solace in the fact that women have proved time and time again, from the first interracial Anti-Slavery Convention of American Women in 1837 to the Women's Convention held by Women's March in Detroit in October 2017, that when people come together, share resources, and turn our daring discussions into opportunities to grow and change, there's nothing we can't do.

So how did the Women's March happen? Let's start at the beginning.

Washington, D.C.

The view down
Pennsylvania Avenue NW.

Washington, D.C.

Participants in Washington, D.C., march with a banner showing the eyes of a woman who was not able to attend, as part of Inside Out, a project created by the artist JR.

Washington, D.C.

BEFORE

Clinton supporters at the
Javits Center in New York City
on election night.

NOV 8–9, 2016

ELECTION NIGHT AND ITS AFTERMATH

"I THINK WE SHOULD MARCH." ON THE NIGHT OF NOVEMBER 8, 2016, WHILE PROCESSING THE OUTCOME OF THE PRESIDENTIAL RACE, TERESA SHOOK, A RETIRED ATTORNEY IN HAWAII, POSTED THOSE FIVE SIMPLE WORDS ON A PRIVATE FACEBOOK GROUP PAGE BEFORE SHE WENT TO BED. BY THE TIME SHE AWOKE THE NEXT MORNING, 10,000 WOMEN HAD HEEDED HER CALL TO ACTION, SIGNING ON TO MARCH. AND AROUND THE COUNTRY, OTHER WOMEN WERE PLOTTING.

TERESA SHOOK
Founder, Women's March

At first I was depressed and felt hopeless. I jumped on Facebook hoping to find some women to commiserate with—to help make sense of what had happened. I got on a thread where women were feeling the same, and the more they expressed hopelessness, the more I felt that old fiery urge to "do something." So I commented that "we should march." One woman in that thread said, "I'm in," and that was all I needed to hear.

I jumped off the Facebook page and went to make a private event. Before I went to bed that night, there were about 40 women attending and another 40 or so who had indicated that they were interested. When I woke up the next day, there were over 10,000 women attending and another 10,000 women interested. I started saying "Oh my God, oh my God" to myself over and over, trying to take it all in. Then I got busy bringing more women on board.

BOB BLAND
Women's March Cochair and
National Organizer

On election night my daughter came in before her bedtime, at like eight o'clock, and said, "Mama, tell Hillary Clinton I'm sorry."

And I was like, "Oh, baby, why? The night's young! There's still a lot of states to come in."

She said, "Yeah, but Hillary Clinton has three—and Donald Trump has twenty-one." Because, see, even though she's six and a half, she can at least read the numbers. I was the one in denial. She knew. She knew exactly what was happening, and I couldn't . . . you know. . . .

Just like everyone else, by 2 A.M. I'm sitting there with my mouth agape, staring at a now-empty screen and thinking, What is my life going to be now, and what am I going to do for my family? I was pregnant at the time and I thought, Oh my God, I'm about to bring another girl into a world where we've just demonstrated that the world's even more sexist than we had imagined. And the most hateful person, the least responsible person, the one that reminds me so much of the people I'm battling at work in the manufacturing world of the fashion industry in New York City right now—someone like that is actually going to be the president of the United States.

So, at this point, I had a few thousand followers in this Facebook group of "nasty women," and they all came to me online the morning after the election saying, "What are we going to do? What are we going to do?" And it just hit me. I was like, Well, we should march on Washington, D.C., on inauguration weekend. And I put it out there.

"THE NEXT 1,459 DAYS OF THE TRUMP ADMINISTRATION WILL BE 1,459 DAYS OF RESISTANCE."

ANGELA DAVIS,
ACTIVIST AND WRITER

ONSTAGE IN WASHINGTON, D.C.

Photographer Kisha Bari was embedded with the march organizers throughout their planning. Here, a meeting in The Gathering for Justice offices.

Within two hours, thanks to the magic of the Internet, my friend in Philadelphia who's also a sustainable-fashion designer called me, and she was like, "Hey, you'll never guess. There's somebody else who is planning a march."

At this time, Teresa's page was called the Million Woman March, and I saw that she had a few thousand more people who said they were going than I did, so I connected with her, and I said, "Hey, Teresa, I just wanted to share with you that I'm also planning a march on Washington that same weekend. Why don't we combine forces?" And between her and some of the other organizers, we were able to merge the pages.

CARMEN PEREZ
Cochair and National Organizer

Teresa didn't feel she had the capacity to organize a march of that caliber. So she gave her blessing to Bob. They consolidated the two events. And then Vanessa Wruble came aboard and in turn reached out to Michael Skolnik, the chair of the board of the nonprofit The Gathering for Justice, to find someone who could organize a march. And Michael said, "I know exactly who you need: Carmen Perez and Tamika Mallory can organize in their sleep."

CASSADY FENDLAY
**Director of Communications
and National Organizer**

It's kind of beautiful how Teresa birthed this idea into the world and let it go. She gave us this idea and didn't want to hold it and control it.

BREANNE BUTLER
**Global Director and
National Organizer**

I got on Facebook and saw a post from a mutual friend, Bob Bland. We had tons of friends in common through the fashion industry, so I messaged her and asked what I could do to help. She said, "I saw you used to work at Facebook. Can you help make Facebook pages for all the states to mobilize to get to D.C.?" This was funny because I was actually working as the executive pastry chef at Facebook New York! But at that point it didn't matter. She added me as a host of the event, which led to a 32-hour love affair with my computer screen. I thought we were going to break Facebook.

VANESSA WRUBLE, Director of Operations and National Organizer The decision to hold the march in January emerged out of Facebook chatter, but what tipped it to the twenty-first, the day *after* the inauguration, was that it was a Saturday; and therefore working people would be more able to attend, and kids would be more able to join, since they didn't have school. It also shifted the feeling of what we were doing out there—we were not going out to shout in the face of would-be inauguration goers and clash with them. We were there to stand calmly together, speaking as one voice.

MY MARCH

"I DON'T THINK I EVER WOULD HAVE CALLED MYSELF AN ACTIVIST."

I didn't think I would go to the Women's March at all—not when I first heard about it. I'm 23 and new to the "real world." I studied feminism as an undergraduate at Cornell, so I was the one that friends texted all night on November 8 as the election results came in: "What do we do?" But I had nothing to offer them. I don't think I ever would have called myself an activist.

By the time January came around I was dejected—this presidency would cast a shadow over the start of my adult life as a woman, working and supporting myself in the same city where Trump came into his fame. In my mind, this election would ruin the lives of people of color, the poor, LGBTQIA+ folk, immigrants, and refugees. But up until the week of the march, I didn't think I would go. I just couldn't. I was still too broken up.

Then, the week of the march, my dad, a 66-year-old white man, came to me and told me I should go—he said I couldn't miss out on this piece of history.

My father came of age during the Vietnam War; he was teargassed during the Hard Hat Riot. He insisted that I go to D.C. and said he'd drive me down himself.

As we drove together, Dad told me about his own experiences with political activism, about what it had changed, and about feeling that his convictions mattered so much that he'd put his body on the line. I couldn't help but feel that he was passing on a torch of some kind to me. Like the responsibility for social change was being transferred from his baby boomer generation to mine, the millennials, at that moment. Now I know I won't let myself or my future children—if I have any—sit out these moments. I know how necessary it is to show up.

JAMIE ZABINSKY
23, New York City, documentary film outreach coordinator; marched in Washington, D.C.

GINNY SUSS, Producer and National Organizer
Vanessa told me there were rumblings of a mass women's march happening on the Internet. She was finding out details, but she asked if I wanted to be involved—we had worked together at OkayAfrica, a media company. I jumped at the chance. I had been devastated by 45's win. It was like looking into Dante's *Inferno* and watching the devils falling into the fiery pit.

I was foreseeing having this fascist, racist, reality-star idiot in office and horrified about what that would mean for immigration, for health care, for reproductive rights. I was thinking about the loss of human rights, the threat to Black Lives Matter, to LGBTQ people, to our education system. I was sort of compelled into action in a way that I hadn't been in a really long time.

Washington, D.C.

EMMA COLLUM
National Field Director and
National Organizer

So the day after the election, I was just tremendously upset. I remember I was thinking about going to have a margarita and just going home and calling it a day. And I saw posts on Facebook about Bob Bland saying that there was going to be a march on Washington.

I Facebooked Bob, and I said, "I'm an attorney. Whatever I can do, I'd love to help." And she wrote me back, and said, "Are you in Florida?" And I said, "I am." And she said, "Do you want to run Florida?" And I said sure, having no idea what that meant, no idea what this was possibly going to be. Eventually I got on a group call with all the other women who at the time had done something similar to what I had done—had just volunteered to run their state, run their local area.

MRINALINI CHAKRABORTY
National Field Director and
National Organizer

I reached out to Bob on Wednesday morning following the election when there were still only like 2,000 or 3,000 people on her page. And I was like, Bob, you don't know me but I really want to help. Please tell me what to do. I'm a pretty good organizer. When I was growing up in India, I fought for the rights of sex workers and victims of human trafficking.

31

National organizer Evvie Harmon (at center, with two hands raised) announces to the team that there will be a march in Antarctica.

I came to this country at 18 all by myself. I can get things started. And so Bob and Breanne and another organizer, I don't remember her name, were getting state chapters started. And they were like, can you start Illinois? Because we don't really have anybody yet. And I said, I don't really know what you need from state chapters, but yes, I can start one in Illinois.

BOB Part of the reason that we were able to launch all of this so quickly is that we ran it kind of like a viral start-up; we made changes on the fly and weren't afraid to fail and try again. And I think that's actually one of the reasons why it was successful—it's all about the moment, you know?

NOV 9–11, 2016

WHAT'S IN A NAME? EVERYTHING.

THE WOMEN'S MARCH FACED ONE OF ITS EARLIEST CHALLENGES WHEN A WAVE OF ONLINE CRITICISM ABOUT THE APPROPRIATION OF THE NAME "MILLION WOMAN MARCH" THREATENED TO PUT AN END TO THE PARTICIPATION OF AFRICAN AMERICAN WOMEN.

Washington, D.C.

BOB In the span of 48 hours, the page says there's 75,000 people interested. And then it was 150,000 people. And soon 250,000 people. The beautiful part of it being viral was all the comments. And then suddenly people started asking things like "Where are the people of color?" and "Where are the Muslims?" And they were going through the lists of people that we were saying that we wanted to march in unity with on the Facebook page, and saying, "Yeah, but where are they in the leadership?" And for the first time, oh wow, we realized that we hadn't really thought about who was going to lead this. We were just organizing as a bunch of people, and it was just like this huge, viral thing. And at that point, people said, "Look, y'all are white. Like, all of y'all." And we were like, "Oh, shit. Yeah, you're right."

VANESSA There was also an uproar about what some people were calling the march at first. They had called it the Million Woman March—being ignorant of the 1997 Million Woman March in Philadelphia, which had focused on uniting and empowering women of color in America. That was one reason why the march was immediately a lightning rod for race dynamics. What we were hearing was basically, "Black women, you should not march with these white women, and this is why." And then it was like, oops, a bunch of ignorant white women have reappropriated this name that black women used in the past. It was a huge controversy.

I reached out to the march group and said, "The name needs to be changed ASAP." Of course, it was not done out of anything but lack of awareness. And I said, "Let's call it the Women's March on Washington." Basically, as an homage to the 1963 March on Washington we all think of when we hear the phrase.

PAOLA MENDOZA, Artistic Director and National Organizer I got a call from Vanessa because they were seeing tremendous pushback, because some people were calling it the Million Woman March. Folks were giving them major

> ## "IF ONE WOMAN SUFFERS, WE ALL SUFFER. AND BELIEVE YOU ME, MY PEOPLE AND MY WOMEN HAVE SUFFERED."
>
> ### JENNY MUNRO, WIRADJURI ELDER AND HUMAN RIGHTS CAMPAIGNER
>
> ### ONSTAGE IN SYDNEY, AUSTRALIA

criticism, saying that this meant it was a white women's march and that women of color, particularly black women, were not welcome historically in the feminist movement, and this was more of the same. Historical conflicts that have existed between black women and white feminists kind of reemerged in this moment in time, where everyone was so angry and hurt and scared.

BOB At that point, I was not an experienced activist or organizer. I said, "OK, we absolutely need to pay attention to the comments and hear what people are saying." All of us were receiving thousands of direct messages on Facebook—way more than we could possibly read. We had a lot of people offering to help too. Thankfully, one of the people calling us out on Facebook was Vanessa Wruble, and she didn't just call out that we didn't have people of color centered in leadership. She said, "Hey, you have to include women of color, and I want to introduce you to some."

VANESSA I saw the opportunity—and this is where you can fault me for being naive and idealistic—but I saw it as an opportunity to try and properly build a coalition amongst women from different backgrounds. I jumped, thinking, I can help make this happen. And I knew that the march needed to be led at least in part by women of color. And those voices needed to be at the forefront of everything that was going on, because we can't continue to make the same mistakes—we can't do something that's going to actually tear this country apart. We can't afford that at all right now.

MICHAEL SKOLNIK, Board Chair of The Gathering for Justice I called 300 to 400 people over those first four or five days after the election, looking for people to take leadership in building an opposition. Like who is the one who's already out of bed at six in the morning and not crying their eyes out and ready to go to work? And I knew that Carmen, Tamika, Linda, and Paola [Michael's

---

MY MARCH

"I THOUGHT ABOUT WHAT WAS REALLY IMPORTANT, AND IT WAS LIBERTY."

I'm an American, but I've lived in London for 25 years. And all that time I have been really rubbish about doing an absentee ballot. In 2016 I finally did—to vote for Hillary. So when Trump was elected, I got a barrage of emails from friends saying "Come to America" to be part of the march. Then when I found out about the London march, I knew I had to go. I got people together to knit pussy hats. And on the day of the march I bought a pink balloon and thought about what is really important to me. And it was liberty—liberty for all people, including the people who supported Trump. I wrote "liberty" on the balloon. Before Trump, families were free to have civilized conversations among Republicans and Democrats, but now it's too awful. Not just politically but also personally.

We went off to the march, to Grosvenor Square near the American embassy. But you couldn't even get near Grosvenor Square. There were women and men and children and people of all shapes and sizes—and dogs. Maybe bringing dogs is a British thing. It was wonderful, but it was also chaos. It was so much bigger than anyone expected. I climbed up on a railing at the Marriott because I was scared of getting crushed. And of terrorism. I had to get out of that crowd, so we ended up—what else?—stopping for tea.

Showing up with my hat and my pink "liberty" balloon was my way of marching. Liberty, to me, says we can have different views without violence or anger. So you can imagine that a male friend's Facebook post following the march surprised me: "Can't the women stay at home and express their views another way? Why do they have to inconvenience the people of London?"

So I replied with what I meant as a lighthearted response: "Another misogynist's cage rattled!" And then he said, "How dare you call me a misogynist?" and asked for a public apology. I refused and said, "I'm hurt and offended because this was about people being able to stand up for their beliefs.

He unfriended me, another relationship severed in this politically seismic new world. And I realized that achieving what I had marched for—the right to have one's views and not have that be divisive—was a lot harder than it looked.

AMY KEMP
50, London, marketing executive; marched in London

partner in life and work] were that type. And so my initial thought was they had to be involved.

TAMIKA MALLORY
Cochair and
National Organizer

The first call we received from anyone at the march was asking us to join the Million Woman March. And the second call we got that same day was that the name had been changed.

CARMEN

Michael Skolnik introduced me to Tamika over the phone, and they said they wanted to center women of color. We agreed to meet up with Vanessa and Ginny and the other organizers. Tamika made sure that Linda [Sarsour] was a part of this with us because we don't do anything without Linda.

And so we met with Bob and the other women. And we took our

A Women's March team meeting. From left: Michael Skolnik, Michelle Minguez, Daveen Trentman, and Genevieve Roth.

WOMEN'S RIGHTS = HUMAN RIGHTS

GIRLS JUST WANNA HAVE FUN-DAMENTAL HUMAN RIGHTS

Los Angeles

binder from the fiftieth anniversary of the March on Washington, because Tamika had been part of organizing that. And I had been there in a supporting role through 1199, the labor union, and also because I work closely with, and have been mentored by, Harry Belafonte.

TAMIKA I had to contact Bernice King, Dr. King's daughter, to get her involved in helping to address the name change, because people were still concerned about appropriation of the Million Woman March name. I had to get her on the phone and ask her to join a call with the organizers and, really, to provide her blessing, so that we could move forward, and she ultimately did do that.

PAOLA We spent a lot of time talking to our own communities, women of color in particular—Latinas, black women, and indigenous women who have typically been marginalized from the feminist movement—to say to them that this was not just a white women's march. For the first time in history on a mass scale, this was going to be a major movement for everyone, that was being led by women of color, and women of color were fighting at the table as leaders. If our communities were not going to join this movement now, when would they? Because this was our opportunity to make sure that our voices would be heard.

NANTASHA WILLIAMS
Deputy of Operations and
National Organizer White women were technically not leading the march. And that's the part of the message that was always missed in this whole entire thing. Women of color were at the planning table. That messaging just never took. People kept on thinking white women were leading this.

LINDA SARSOUR
Cochair and National
Organizer Black women have embraced me, helped me grow, educated me on important histories that I was not exposed to, and taught me to organize from a place of radical love. They have also challenged me, and through that I have become a better activist and organizer. I truly believe those closest to the pain are closest to the solution, and black women will lead us to the solutions and to justice.

TABITHA
ST. BERNARD-JACOBS
Youth Ambassador Director
and National Organizer For some of us who are of color, there are things that are coming out into the open now that we have been dealing with for a very long time. I came to this country from Trinidad when I was 19, about 15 years ago, and I realized then for the first time in my life that I was a black woman because there's such a stark sort of placement in this country that is assigned according to the color of your skin.

So I was not surprised that Trump was elected president. I was disappointed for sure, and I was sort of shell-shocked; I had been hoping that the country would surprise me. But I distinctly remember having conversations before the election with people who were telling me, "No, this will never happen," and I remember saying, "It is a possibility. I think this country is that racist. It could happen. There are some really racist people in this country."

We were fortunate that some of the white women who were involved in the organizing were aware and were willing to listen to us and that

"WE WILL NOT GO BACK! WE WILL NOT LET THEM TAKE THE RIGHTS OF WOMEN WHO HAVE FOUGHT FOR SO MANY DECADES."

DOLORES HUERTA, LABOR LEADER AND CIVIL RIGHTS ACTIVIST

ONSTAGE IN PARK CITY, UTAH

women of color were at the center of organizing this march. But it was definitely a work in progress.

JANAYE INGRAM, Director of Logistics and National Organizer I grew up in Camden, New Jersey, a city that has achieved a reputation for being rough. Growing up there, I was surrounded by the destruction that the systems of oppression in this country created. The night of the election I cried myself to sleep at the prospect of what it meant that our country would elect someone like Donald Trump. I hoped to wake to a new reality, but it wasn't so. I felt like I had to do something—my life experience taught me that each one of us has power and you gain nothing by standing on the sidelines. I had been the lead organizer of the fiftieth anniversary of the March on Washington and had planned other marches, rallies, and demonstrations. When I heard about a march for women, I knew that I needed to be involved, for myself and to make sure that the voices and issues of black women were heard. I agreed to lead the organizing and had no idea that it would be my own rebirth into a new movement.

CARMEN In the days after the election, I didn't know how to engage in conversation with white women, because we had heard that so many white women had voted for Trump. I work in the racial justice world, inside prisons with people who are incarcerated and formerly incarcerated. I work around stopping police brutality. I have learned a lot through my 20 years as a community organizer, and I am also committed to and love my people—Latinx folks. So when I was approached about the march, I saw that as my opportunity to make sure that the communities that I work with—predominantly African American, Latino, poor white, Asian-Pacific Islander—were at the center of what would become the Women's March on Washington. And having studied Chicana feminism, I knew the value of bringing people together—regardless of what specific issue they cared about—and really thinking about how we could intersect, how we could have an inclusive and intersectional movement.

Teresa Shook (center) at the march command center with logistics team member Daria Hall.

March organizers De'Ara Balenger, Tamika Mallory, Meredith Shepherd, and Linda Sarsour.

Washington, D.C.

BY JILL SOLOWAY

TO GO OR NOT TO GO?

Jill Soloway is a comedian, writer, and director and the Emmy-winning creator, writer, executive producer, and director of *Transparent*.

I remember the first Facebook post that popped up, a friend saying "We're going to march." And soon everyone was saying "We're going to march."

But then, almost immediately, another friend said, "They don't have a permit. None of this is real. Don't go. I'm not going."

Now, I'm the kind of person who's always wandering around saying "Let's have a revolution! Let's go out in the street and demonstrate!" I say that every other Tuesday under normal circumstances. But my friend saying that they didn't have a permit was enough to stop me in my tracks. And as a Jewish person over age 50, I focus on bathrooms. Which is why I don't go to Burning Man or Coachella. *Where am I going to pee?*

"I'm not going," I said. "I can't go. This thing is going to be a clusterfuck."

Even worse than the bathroom issue was the infighting. I was surprised—I didn't know the name Million Woman March was already taken, and that it was specific to the black community. This idea that at first had seemed so great became a huge problem in an instant. Not only was there no permit, but the march was also racist, a fuck-up in all regards.

I thought to myself, You know what? It's good that I never believed in a revolution because it's too hard anyway. I'm staying home.

But then . . . I watched something happen: On social media, no less, where nothing real ever really happens. I started to see people on my Instagram feed posting pictures *from the Women's March office*. There was ShiShi Rose and Sarah Sophie Flicker and they were all in the same room, and they had amazing art and great branding and whoa!

Something had been fixed. They'd figured it out. Rather than falling apart under the weight of the challenges, they were rising. I was ready to root for the march again. Maybe this could be everyone's march. But there was still a problem.

The march was at the same time as Sundance, and my show *I Love Dick* was premiering there. Maybe *I Love Dick* could be my feminist contribution, maybe the emails going around about setting up a march in Park City would work out and I could skip D.C.

Another day passed. The days were coming fast and furious and people were talking about pink pussy hats. Every single person who had been like "I'm not going" was suddenly going. My sister-in-law in Virginia was going. People in New York were taking the train down. But even if I could move my Sundance dates around, I had a new problem: How do you go from L.A. to D.C. to Utah in two days? This is also something that Jewish people don't do. A five-hour flight means you have to stay for one week. You can't go for one day. It's not allowed.

As the date grew closer, my head was spinning with how I couldn't make this plane flight work, and I couldn't imagine being out on the streets in D.C. without a bathroom, and I can't figure out how to deal with my travel anxiety. *But* I can't miss this day. I can't let this day happen and say I wasn't there. I want to be there and I'm going to go . . . and I'm going to take my son Isaac, who is 20 and needs to have this in his memory bank too. I'm going to take my son, and I'll move mountains to be there.

And at that moment it was an absolute. I was going. I needed to prove to myself that I believed in revolution, that my body mattered, and that I

EVERY SINGLE PERSON WHO HAD BEEN LIKE "I'M NOT GOING" WAS SUDDENLY GOING.

could take my body—this one body that had been witness to decades of patriarchy thieving me out of my power and protagonism—and put it in the streets.

This was four days before the march. Within 12 hours I had booked my hotel room and I had purchased four pink pussy hats from Amazon and then collected 10 more from friends. I was stockpiling pussy hats in bulk, terrified that none of the ones I ordered would be there in time. It was like eclipse glasses. Or fidget spinners. We were all getting them and we were getting them *right now*.

And then everybody was going. And suddenly my son and I were at the airport, waiting to get the flight, and all my friends were there. And we all had our hats on. On the airplane we all took photo after photo of ourselves crowding into rows. The flight attendants were on our side. The seat belt rules seemed to have been waived. We were on our way.

CATS AGAINST PUSSY GRABBING

STAND UP TO RACISM

NO TO

London

At the march offices, Carmen Perez leads fellow organizers in the Assata chant.

NOV 11–14, 2016

THE TEAM EXPANDS

AS MEDIA COVERAGE OF THE NATIONAL AND LOCAL MARCH DETAILED THE ORGANIZERS' PLANS TO MARCH FROM THE LINCOLN MEMORIAL TO THE WHITE HOUSE THE DAY AFTER THE INAUGURATION, THE RAPIDLY GROWING GROUP OF MARCH ORGANIZERS REALIZED THEY HAD LESS THAN TEN WEEKS TO PULL OFF THE EVENT. THEY RECRUITED SEASONED SOCIAL JUSTICE ACTIVISTS, FIRST-TIME ORGANIZERS, SOCIAL ENTREPRENEURS, FASHION DESIGNERS, CHEFS, ARTISTS, AND STRATEGISTS TO GET IT DONE.

Washington, D.C.

MICHAEL SKOLNIK   This thing needed to be housed inside a nonprofit organization, so we offered The Gathering for Justice, which Harry Belafonte started 10 years ago to advance racial justice and end child incarceration.

CARMEN   The risk that I put The Gathering for Justice through as fiscal sponsor of the march stressed me out. I worried my organization could become a target of unnecessary scrutiny by the new administration, or even by people who perpetuated hateful and bigoted views. But I believed that the connection to The Gathering for Justice grounded the Women's March in history. Connecting the two was the right thing to do, even though there were moments of fear.

PAOLA   The organizers came together naturally. No one was interviewed for a job. Folks just brought on the people they knew would get the job done.

When I first heard about the march right after Trump was elected president, I knew that I could not sit and do nothing. I knew that I had to protect the country that had given me so much, not for myself but for the next generation of immigrants coming to follow their dreams.

I was three years old when I immigrated to the U.S. from Colombia. My mom, brother, and I arrived in L.A. to be reunited with my father and start our American dream. Unfortunately, after only a few months, my dad decided he couldn't handle the responsibility, and he abandoned us. We were homeless for a little while, and then my mom ended up getting public housing and finding a job at a fast-food restaurant. Eventually she went to community college. The beauty of America is that as an immigrant who was once homeless, fatherless, and penniless, I was able to be a part of organizing the largest demonstration in the history of the world!

Leading up to the election, Michael and I had been working extremely hard to get Hillary elected. We crisscrossed the country with our son Mateo Ali, canvassing. We kept joking to one another that on November 9 we could rest, because Hillary would be president and we could take a vacation.

DE'ARA BALENGER Women's March Strategic Adviser and National Organizer Sarah Sophie [Flicker] called me and said,

"IT'S INCOMPREHENSIBLE TO ME . . . HOW MILLIONS OF AMERICANS COULD VOTE AGAINST 11 MILLION IMMIGRANT FAMILIES."

HINA NAVEED, COFOUNDER, STATEN ISLAND DREAM COALITION

ONSTAGE IN WASHINGTON, D.C.

"Listen, you know, Tamika and Linda and Carmen . . . they may need help with this march." And I'm like, "What are you even talking about?" I was in Mexico after having worked as national engagement director for Hillary Clinton.

Sarah Sophie said, "Just get on this call with Tamika." So Meredith [Shepherd, whom De'Ara worked with on the Clinton campaign] and I get on this call with Tamika. And our attitude was: Of course we'll be helpful, we want to be involved. What do you guys need us to do?

MEREDITH SHEPHERD, Women's March Strategic Adviser and National Organizer The initial thing that I did was work on helping to build the team—my background is in corporate human resources. I had worked on the Clinton campaign with people who were really amazing at what they did, and I just didn't want them to feel defeated. Part of it was that I didn't want to feel like that dead soldier on the battlefield. I really didn't want them to feel that way either. So many Clinton folks worked on the Women's March: Jenna Lauter, Stephanie Miliano, Reshma Saujani, and many more. To me, to keep fighting and to claim the day after his inauguration was very important.

EMMA Breanne and Bob asked if I would join the national team and run all 50 of the states. Mrinalini and I began working late nights, helping local Women's March organizers in all 50 states get to D.C. for January 21. I ended up working through walking pneumonia because I think I just wanted to channel all of the grief, all of the energy, everything I had that had been riding on this incredible woman becoming president, into the march.

Through all of it, I had, and still have, a full-time job as a lawyer. I would leave my office and go hide behind office dumpsters or go hide behind my car at a lunch break, so that I could make these calls to make this happen. I used all of my spare time, and some of it that wasn't my spare time. And I'm not the only one on the team who was doing that.

NANTASHA I reached out to say, "Hey, do you need help?" And Tamika tells me, "Yes, I need a *lot* of help. Can you come to the office?" I thought it was gonna be simple, like me

---

MY MARCH

"IT FELT LIKE THE BIRTH OF OUR OWN 21ST-CENTURY REVOLUTION."

As a trans girl of color, I knew that the elevation of the antiequality ideologies represented by Trump, his cabinet, and the conservative majority in Congress would have drastic negative effects on my life.

On the morning of the march, I woke up early and I got ready to march for my rights. Before leaving, I swallowed the little turquoise pill that my life depends on: estrogen. So many trans people don't have access to hormones and other medical supports. So many girls like me are afraid to come out, to ask for help, don't know where to get help, are pushed out of schools and homes and forced into dangerous situations just in order to be female in the ways we must be in order to be ourselves. I'm lucky: My parents support me wholeheartedly.

My mom and my best friend and I met up early that morning with a group from the National Center for Transgender Equality at a park behind the Rayburn House Office Building on Capitol Hill. After the march started and we got closer to the route and I saw all the people, I was overwhelmed by the enormity of it. The crowd was huge! We couldn't even move. The streets of Washington, D.C., were saturated with people and signs and chants and love . . . and pussy hats! Pink pussy hats are a bit problematic for trans girls and women and girls of color—I wanted to take people aside and explain that having a vagina and a uterus are not the only things that define us as women and girls. We are women no matter cis or trans, no matter vagina or not, uterus or not, breasts or not. We all walk in different ways, but what unites us is our love and our compassion and our determination to stand up for our rights and the rights of all women. But those hats did serve as a vision that showed unity for that day.

There were so many people everywhere who, like me, were born after 2000. From what I saw at the march, people in my age group were the most diverse racially and ethnically and held the most LGBTQ signs and colors. I was so proud of us! It felt like the birth of our own 21st-century revolution—the first giant leap in the rest of our fantastic lives.

GRACE DOLAN-SANDRINO
16, Washington, D.C., student/advocate;
marched in Washington

helping her with little emails or something. Something where I could just do it from home, or whatever. I have sort of a different approach than a lot of people that are in the Women's March space. I come from a more structured background in government; this was more chaotic. I got to the office, and I saw all these different types of women, and the energy was just super intense. And I thought, What the hell is going on here?

Tamika took me to dinner that evening. And she said, "I really need your help. I really, really, really, really need your help." I was like, "Well, I'm trying to find a job. I could help you a little bit." And she was like, "No. I don't—not a little bit of help. I need you to . . . suspend your *life*. Can you suspend your life and help me? I'll make sure you're good. Can you just, please, until January 21, until this march is over?"

SARAH SOPHIE FLICKER
Women's March Strategic Adviser and National Organizer

Michael Skolnik put me on an email with Tamika, Linda, and Carmen. I had already been involved in things that Tamika and Linda had organized. I had never met Carmen, but I was an admirer of hers and had been to a lot of her rallies and seen all the amazing stuff she was doing. It was funny, because Michael put me on that email and then Tamika and I were on the phone that very night.

My mother's grandfather was the prime minister of Denmark during World War II. The story goes that when the Germans invaded Denmark, my great-grandfather told the king to wear a Jewish star in solidarity with the Jewish community. And then the police force put on stars, as did much of the non-Jewish Danish population, so that the Nazi soldiers found it hard to distinguish Jews from non-Jews. I grew up hearing that story; it was a lesson in solidarity and civil disobedience.

JENNA ARNOLD
Women's March Strategic Adviser and National Organizer

Michael is a really great model of what a male ally can look like. He put a lot of us together and then just completely stepped away. When Paola called me and said, "Yeah, we're working on the march" and listed my sisters who were participating, I was like, Oh my God, this is going to be a thing. Paola told me they needed help raising money. I'm a social entrepreneur, and I've built a bunch of for-profit and nonprofit companies in the social sector. I was at the United Nations for many years. I've created a bunch of television shows and films to get people to give a shit about important causes. So I came on board.

JANAYE

A "leaderful" movement is a movement where there isn't a single person whose vision creates the strategy, but rather many people who can be visionary leaders. Ideas and power converge into something more powerful than what one leader could do on their own. It is like the force of a fist versus an individual finger. Women's March is a perfect example of a leaderful movement. While we had four cochairs who represented various communities, there were many other leaders at the table there to create something more beautiful and powerful than what any of us could have done alone.

March organizers (from left): Nantasha Williams, Breanne Butler, Ting Ting Cheng, Bob Bland, Janaye Ingram, Paola Mendoza, Carmen Perez, Sarah Sophie Flicker, Tamika Mallory, and Tabitha St. Bernard-Jacobs.

Washington, D.C.

MY SISTERS' KEEPER

BY MELANIE L. CAMPBELL

Melanie L. Campbell is the convener of the Black Women's Roundtable, an intergenerational network that champions just and equitable public policy on behalf of black women.

In late November 2016, I received a call from Tamika Mallory, my sister in the civil rights and social justice movement, asking me what I thought about the Women's March. My initial response was silence because what I had heard up to this point was that the march was not about black women, that white women were leading it out of guilt for voting for Donald Trump. So I shared a few choice words that expressed my sentiments: I did not support the Women's March, because as far as I was concerned, our white sisters were only calling for a march to rid themselves of the guilt of voting for a sexist who was supported by racists, like David Duke. As a black woman who was part of the 94 percent who voted for Hillary Clinton, I felt like my white sisters had abandoned us, choosing race over gender. I was tired, mad as hell, and didn't feel I needed to support their march to make them feel better.

Then Tamika told me that she and several other sisters of color had taken on leadership roles to organize the Women's March alongside one of its original creators. She also shared that another sister leader in the movement, Janaye Ingram, had agreed to take on the role of organizing the logistics for the Women's March. In that moment, none of us knew the Women's March would go down in history as the largest women's march in the U.S.

I asked Tamika why she felt compelled to take this on. Was she willing to put her reputation on the line? I had worked with her for many years through the Black Women's Roundtable. Becoming a leader of the Women's March meant that she would be utilizing the trust she had built with friends and colleagues to sign on to a march that was not supported by a majority of black women leaders at the time. I remember vividly how she spoke with discernment and a clarity of purpose: She understood the stakes and felt it was her responsibility to step up for those black women who had paved the way for her generation to lead.

I felt her passion and quickly saw that it was vital that black women not only participate in the Women's March but also, more crucially, be in the leadership and central to defining its agenda. Mentors like civil rights activist Dorothy I. Height had guided and supported me, and in that moment I could hear my sister ancestors challenging me to "pay it forward." So I let go of my frustration, disappointment, and anger. If I truly believed that "I am my sisters' keeper," I had to step up and support my sisters.

My next question was, "So how can I help?" I wish I hadn't asked! "We need your help getting black women to endorse and participate in the Women's March," Tamika told me. I told her it wouldn't be easy because the narrative was that this march was not about black women.

But I was in, so off we went: I called on three of my own mentors (Cora Masters Barry, Clayola Brown, and Dr. Barbara Williams-Skinner). I leaned on the sister shield and asked for their help to reach out and encourage black women to support the march. They didn't hesitate, and we got to work and were successful in securing endorsements from several civil rights and black women–led organizations.

Although the presence of black women at the march wasn't ultimately what I had hoped, undoubtedly many of those who were there had decided to attend after they could see themselves in the leadership and witness that issues important to women of color were central to the march agenda. That made all the late-night phone calls, hard conversations, and in some cases strained relationships worthwhile.

On the morning of the Women's March, I woke up feeling we were about to witness history. Little did I know it would be the largest march ever. I am grateful to God for speaking to my spirit when I got that call from Tamika, urging me to walk by faith and be my sisters' keeper.

NOV 17–19, 2016

MIDWIFING A MOVEMENT

ONCE ORGANIZERS LINDA SARSOUR, CARMEN PEREZ, AND TAMIKA MALLORY CONFIRMED THAT THEY WOULD JOIN THE MARCH TEAM AS COCHAIRS, THE PLANNING BEGAN IN EARNEST. BUT FIRST, BOB HAD A BABY.

BOB   The beauty of working with women is that we're very collaborative. And it was just so great to see that women felt that all was not lost and that together we could still make the future that we dreamed of for our children.

       Within like three or four days of meeting, we had a permit application in, we had written a manifesto that went up on the website and on social media. And then I went into labor. And it was like, Wait, wait! This is not supposed to happen for three weeks. Or two weeks, or something like that. I knew I wasn't supposed to have this baby until after Thanksgiving, for sure.

Washington, D.C.

BREANNE I hopped on the 5 train to Brooklyn and went to the hospital. I found Bob and Michael Foulger, her husband, and gave them both a hug. Then I sat on the hospital floor for the next five hours with my computer. I was trying to get all of the information from Bob about what she had been working on so that her work wouldn't stop after the baby. It was insane.

BOB Tamika came to the hospital too. Literally the second time I'm ever meeting her, I'm in active labor in the hospital. We had a two-hour meeting. We'd talk for a few minutes and then I'd [*mimicking labor noise*]. She was there basically within hours of Chloe being born. And she and Chloe have a really special relationship as a result of that. I was in labor for like 40 hours. And it felt like a week, because people kept on calling me, like they wouldn't hear that I was in labor, you know? It was like, "Bob, we need this, we need that, we need this—this is what's going on." But because I had had problems with my first pregnancy, with my first daughter, eventually I had to have my husband get on the phone to say, "Don't call her until we tell you."

MICHAEL Carmen and Tamika were running back and forth to the hospital. But that night they struck a deal, agreeing that they would come on as cochairs of the march. Bob had her baby. And they all became one team. Including Bob's baby, whom she brought to the march two months later.

JANAYE Little Chloe, Bob's baby, she's like our mascot. You know, other organizers have children and daughters who are older than Chloe. But I think the thing that we always think about when we look at Chloe is that we don't want to pass this torch on to her. We don't want her to have to carry the mantle of fighting oppression. I think maybe that's a little idealistic, but I don't want her to have to fight the same fights that we're fighting. There will always be more fights and other fights and newer fights. But I don't want her to have to fight through these same fights.

SARAH SOPHIE Every time I stopped and thought about it, Bob's situation while we

"WE STAND SHOULDER TO SHOULDER TO MAKE CLEAR: WE ARE HERE! WE WILL NOT BE SILENT! WE WILL NOT PLAY DEAD!"

SENATOR ELIZABETH WARREN OF MASSACHUSETTS

ONSTAGE IN BOSTON

Baby Chloe in the arms of her mother, Bob Bland, photographed by Amber Mahoney during a visit to the Women's March offices.

were planning the march just floored me, because I have three kids, so I know what that time in life is like. And it's incredible that Bob did what she did.

BOB   Now Chloe is the "march baby" because she was born on the nineteenth of November, and we can count how long it's been since we all met each other by how old she is.

NOV 19– DEC 15, 2016

PLANS, PERMITS, DRAMA

FROM ITS INCEPTION, THE WOMEN'S MARCH ENCOUNTERED QUESTIONS AND CONCERNS ABOUT THE STATUS OF ITS PERMIT, INSURANCE, AND A CONFIRMED NATIONAL MALL LOCATION. SOCIAL MEDIA BUZZED WHEN *THE WASHINGTON POST* REPORTED THAT THE DEMONSTRATION WAS ORIGINALLY PLANNED TO BE IN FRONT OF THE LINCOLN MEMORIAL BUT WOULD HAVE TO MOVE TO AN ALTERNATE LOCATION.

A
WOMANS
PLACE
IS   IN
THE
RESISTANCE

Washington, D.C.

CASSADY At the beginning, no one knew the march was going to be an epic thing. I had been communications director for other national mobilizations, and I thought I knew what I was getting into. When we first took it up, we thought, Oh, it would be great if we could get, like, 200,000 people in D.C. We could probably do that, right? [*Laughs*.]

There were so many forces working against it. Isn't that what virtually all organizing is? The media was not interested in anything but the permit. People had all these doubts. What was this thing really about? And they'd say, "You know, I heard they don't have a permit."

GLORIA STEINEM
Honorary Cochair I caught the excitement of the march idea in the same way so many did—hearing it in the street and in an online explosion of energy. This was in response to the perfect storm of the 2016 presidential election. Trump, an unsuccessful businessman who became a TV brand name, was an unqualified presidential candidate. He actually lost the election by more than 10 million votes, nearly three to Hillary Clinton and almost eight to other candidates. He only won because of the electoral college, itself a remnant from the days when slave owners demanded additional electoral votes based on the number of slaves in their state.

I was distracted worrying about march logistics. I knew from past marches on Washington—also Chicago and Detroit and other cities—how complicated mass events can be. The initial organizers hadn't been through the long process of getting public permits, police protection, and fleets of buses, not to mention plotting a march route and staging areas, plus Porta-Potties. People with experience began volunteering their knowledge, but I still worried and emailed myself into a stew.

PAOLA Yeah, it became a story that we didn't have a permit. It began with a Facebook post that went viral. This was clearly just someone trying to throw a wrench in things, and it seemed as if we couldn't get over and get ahead of the story about the permit. It was just nonstop every day when we were talking to potential partners, and they'd ask, "What's up with the permit?" "Do you have a permit?"

What we couldn't seem to get across to partners was that there were other

> **"ONE OF US CAN BE DISMISSED. TWO OF US CAN BE IGNORED. BUT TOGETHER WE ARE A MOVEMENT AND WE ARE UNSTOPPABLE."**
>
> **CECILE RICHARDS, PRESIDENT, PLANNED PARENTHOOD FEDERATION OF AMERICA**
>
> **ONSTAGE IN WASHINGTON, D.C.**

marches planned for January 21, like Bikers for Trump. The irony was that no one was asking them about their permit.

SARAH SOPHIE   We were getting slammed with the hoopla around the permits, and really it was thinly veiled sexism. I remember being in the office and Linda was on some call, and at one point she was like, "Did anyone ask Martin Luther King Jr. if he had a permit? I'm just wondering."

MICHAEL   David Simas, who was a senior adviser to President Obama, reached out to me and said, "Look, we want to make sure everything is OK. We hear you're involved in the Women's March, and we want to make sure you all are OK, and we're hearing that you can't get a permit." And I said, "Janaye Ingram has it under control. The permit will be fine."

I connected David and Janaye, just in case they needed help from the administration. (For the record, they didn't.) I wanted to make sure that if they needed help, if they needed doors to be opened that I could open, that I would be there for them. And not just for that moment but for the rest of their lives.

DE'ARA   Tamika brings it up all the time. They constantly questioned the permit. Even the women's organizations were like, "Where's all of y'all's permits?" No one did that to Al Sharpton, and he marched before us.

But that's what we do to women and that's what we do to women's movements, and it's just fascinating to me—and I think of Hillary.

Why aren't we talking about how it is almost impossible to function as a woman leader in America? When we think of characteristics of leaders, all the words are synonymous with men. How can women operate and be successful as leaders on the same level as men in that environment?

CASSADY   When we got our permit, on December 15, it was such a big deal that *The Washington Post* broke the story.

MY MARCH

"THERE ARE NO STREETS IN ANTARCTICA!"

It was my third trip as a tourist to my favorite place on the planet. The ice glows blue from the inside there. But in the nine years since I'd last been to Antarctica, penguin colonies had been dying, and I could see enormous changes in the glaciers, even with my untrained eye. I was in mourning because I was afraid that the damage the president might do to the earth would be irreversible.

I'm from Oakland, a liberal/progressive area. I had been moderately active in terms of donating, but I had never closed down streets. This time was different. I wanted to fight this. I decided I was going to do my own Women's March in Antarctica, with a focus on the environment and peace. I tried to register on the Women's March site, but it needed a street address and zip code. There are no streets in Antarctica! There are no zip codes! It's a three-day boat ride from the tip of South America. Eventually I called, and the organizers helped register me. With Antarctica, the Women's March happened on seven continents.

I brought paper and pens to make signs, and I gave a presentation to everyone on the ship and the crew—174 people, mostly tourists from New Zealand, Australia, the U.S., Canada, England, and the Philippines. The response was amazing. Many women said they had been sad they couldn't participate in the marches at home and were so happy we were planning our own. One woman had already knitted a pussy hat. Just that first discussion made us feel there was more hope in the world—if we couldn't have hope in our government.

We took a group picture on Friday, and, amazingly, the sun came out and the wind broke just in time. We talked to an Argentinean guy from the research station who wanted to march with us, which took some of the sting out of the inauguration. On the day of the march, we marched single file in a path, holding signs, up to a ridge. Most of us were chanting "Save the planet! Save Antarctica! Save the penguins!" Others just cheered. It was so powerful.

LINDA ZUNAS
42, Oakland, California, analytics manager;
marched in Antarctica

Los Angeles

Neko Harbor, Antarctica

Washington, D.C.

BY AI-JEN POO

A WOMAN'S WORK IS NEVER DONE (IN A DEMOCRACY)

About five years ago, I heard the social movement historian Frances Fox Piven speak. She described the activist campaigns she was observing at the time—the DREAMers, the Fight for $15, and Occupy Wall Street (and I'm sure she would add Black Lives Matter now)—as early signals of the coming of the country's next great social movement. This new movement would engage millions and fundamentally transform our democracy, in the way that the civil rights movement and the labor movement of the 1930s had before. At the time, I wondered how we would know when the movement had arrived.

On January 21, 2017, my question was answered.

The Women's March was not just a march. Anyone who marched will tell you that. It was a moment in history when our nation's very soul was in question. It was one of those times in history when we are called to work harder and take greater risk, not just for our families but for the future of the nation.

On the streets of Washington, I saw millions of everyday women taking responsibility for our future: mothers, grandmothers, women of every faith, professionals, women who had never marched before, women who had marched for every issue under the sun, little girls marching for the first time. Women coming together—as women have for centuries throughout cultures around the world.

As I looked at the masses of women around me, these names rang through my mind:

Sojourner Truth	Audre Lorde
Susan B. Anthony	Wilma Mankiller
Ella Baker	Dorothy Bolden
Sylvia Rivera	

These women stood up in years past. They marched, they asserted their humanity and dignity against the odds, they understood, they

Ai-jen Poo is director of the National Domestic Workers Alliance and codirector of Caring Across Generations, a coalition of advocacy organizations working to transform the long-term care system in the U.S.

organized, and built power; they voted (or fought for the right to vote) and they changed the course of history.

We learn about precious few of these women in school. Some are known mainly to activists, and countless more only in their local communities. While many people associate women's work with caring and cleaning, if we look a little closer at the history of this nation, we see that defending and expanding democracy is, and always has been, women's work. As part of every major social movement through the generations, women have been at the heart of bringing our democracy forward, closer to the dream of equality and opportunity for all.

Among those women marching on Washington were domestic workers, home care workers, and family caregivers, many of them members of the National Domestic Workers Alliance, which I cofounded in 2007. They are the unsung heroines who help us look after the most precious parts of our lives—our children, our aging loved ones, people with disabilities, and our homes. Many are immigrants and women of color. As people who care both for their own families and for others' families, they are in a position to know when we have an emergency on our hands. If you asked anyone marching with the domestic-worker contingent that day why they marched, they might talk about immigration, health care, or violence against women. Or they might simply say, "Because our democracy is in crisis and it needs our care."

A woman's work is never done when our democracy is at stake.

Since the march, many have asked whether the moment has been lost. But look more closely and you will see that women are the ones continuing to show up for one another, at town hall meetings, at the airports, after a life was lost near a white supremacists' rally in Charlottesville, Virginia. Women continue to be the first responders to crises in our democracy and otherwise.

Now, imagine women voters electing thousands of women and pro-gender-equity candidates to office in 2018, building toward a moment of truth in 2020 when we make this administration a tiny blip in the arc of history. It is our generational responsibility to step forward and make this moment one that is remembered as a correction in favor of our democracy. And the Women's March, and the culture in the street that day, carry important lessons for us about *how* we win.

The march was multigenerational and multiracial. People who marched were kind toward one another. Marchers carried signs across a broad spectrum of issues, everything from health care and abortion access to good jobs and higher wages. From criminal justice reform and immigrant rights to peace and climate change. From child care and education to elder care and housing. There was room for it all. There was no need to choose what you were most in favor of. No hierarchy of human value. No one and no issue didn't belong.

When women are presented with violence and hate, we are kind and caring. When division and derision surround us, we challenge each other to be better. We have done it time and time again.

The march was the start of the movement this nation deserves. Because that's what women do.

Lansing, Michigan

Los Angeles

BY SISTER AISHA
AL-ADAWIYA

SANKOFA: LOOK BACK TO MOVE FORWARD

Sister Aisha al-Adawiya is
the founder of Women in
Islam, Inc., an organization
of Muslim women focused
on human rights and social
justice.

It always excites me to see younger generations of people, especially women, making the sacrifices they must make in order to bring about change, as the organizers of the Women's March did leading up to that January day. Whenever I speak to young people who are involved in movement struggles, I try to remind them that some of the challenges they are facing are new, but many are not new. I speak from experience. I'm 74 years young. I grew up in the segregated and unequal South in Alabama, where I witnessed discrimination up close and personal. Daily life meant navigating structural racism for survival. I made my way to New York City in my twenties. I eventually found Islam and was inspired by Malcolm X. So I have watched movements form and shape-shift over the decades.

It is important to make the time to go back and learn from history, to understand the struggles that others have gone through, and to build on their successes and learn from their mistakes. You don't have to reinvent the wheel every time. There is a Ghanaian word for this process of looking back to move forward: *sankofa*. Although we have generation gaps on one level, on a deeper level there is continuity, and if younger people and elders reach out to one another, we can bridge the divide.

The young people who are now on the forefront of this movement are standing on the shoulders of those who went before them, even as they are developing new ideas and using new technology. The challenges they encountered were to be expected. Within the feminist discourse there has historically been this problem of finding inclusivity, and that became an issue again with this march. Racism is a part of our culture. We have to acknowledge this in order to overcome it.

The organizers of the Women's March made efforts to address not only racism but also the issue of how Islamic women—and religious women in general—are represented. That too has always been a challenge within the movement. The exclusion of the LGBT community has also been an issue, but these communities emerged to have a more powerful voice in the march. The next step is to include more of the Native American voice. It's just amazing that somehow their struggle, an ongoing genocide, has totally escaped us.

Another challenge we see down through history is the struggle to stay true to a clearly stated mission. It's one thing to show up for a march, but what is the ideology behind it, the vision? You march in the streets and show your resistance. But then what? This march may have started with Trump, but history teaches us that it's not just about him— he is just one individual, a symptom of a much deeper malady within our society. In addition to protesting the things we are against, we need to find a way to magnify what it is that we are *for*. It's easy to tear down, but it's much harder to build.

Sankofa essentially means "go back and get it." And if we go back through history we will see that a movement needs to be something that is owned by the people. We live in a culture that teaches us to be individualistic, and we're starstruck by the one with the most hits on Twitter or Facebook. But when we elevate people to rock-star levels, the

IN ORDER TO KNOW WHERE YOU ARE GOING, YOU HAVE TO KNOW WHERE YOU ARE COMING FROM.

rest of us feel we can relax and let them do the speaking. We've learned these hard lessons through the loss of many of our brilliant, courageous leaders who were brutally taken from us. We need to stay involved. Otherwise the movement is just smoke and mirrors. It looks great from a distance, but when you get back to the local communities, the same old stuff is happening. People are still fighting, suffering, struggling.

In order to know where you are going, you have to know where you are coming from. For people who are given the honor and the responsibility of leadership, *sankofa* becomes part of the agenda, and our leaders must make sure it is included in every aspect of the work, so that everybody can benefit from historical perspective. Future generations have a right to live in a world that sustains and inspires them and supports them in every way. We can't leave a mess for them to clean up. If there is one thing we know from history, it is that they too will have challenges of their own.

DEC 16–28, 2016

BACKERS JOIN. THE BENCH GROWS.

AS DECEMBER PROGRESSED, CIVIL AND HUMAN RIGHTS ORGANIZATIONS INCLUDING PLANNED PARENTHOOD FEDERATION OF AMERICA, NATURAL RESOURCES DEFENSE COUNCIL, AMNESTY INTERNATIONAL, AND THE NATIONAL ASSOCIATION FOR THE ADVANCEMENT OF COLORED PEOPLE CAME ON AS OFFICIAL MARCH PARTNERS. THEIR ENDORSEMENTS GAVE FURTHER LEGITIMACY TO THE MARCH FOR ORGANIZATIONS, DONORS, AND INDIVIDUALS WHO WERE STILL DECIDING WHETHER TO GET INVOLVED.

> ## "WHENEVER YOU FEEL IN DOUBT, WHENEVER YOU WANT TO GIVE UP, YOU MUST ALWAYS REMEMBER TO CHOOSE FREEDOM OVER FEAR."
>
> **JANELLE MONÁE,**
> **SINGER AND SONGWRITER**
>
> **ONSTAGE IN WASHINGTON, D.C.**

CARMEN One of my first calls was to the AFL-CIO because we needed the union members' support on the ground on march day, and I said, "I need your help." Workers have always been central to major movements.

The partner conversations started around seven in the morning, and Paola and I were having conversations every half hour with a new organization or group of people. And every single day we would get on a mass partner call to kinda update where we were—and that would be a conference call with 80 people from different organizations. Or I would be on a call at 11 P.M. with my face on a screen with 200 people in the room.

Paola and I created a dynamic team of about 8 to 10 folks that supported us in the partnerships. But we were the ones having conversations every half hour with a new organization or a new group of people. We had learned from Bernice King that Coretta Scott King had gotten 500 partners for the original March on Washington, and so we had that in our minds as a goal.

LINDA Planned Parenthood came on as one of our premier partners, and Gloria Steinem and Harry Belafonte had come on as honorary cochairs. We were able to make those two announcements to the press. That's when all of the partnerships snowballed.

CARMEN When I first told Mr. B that I was one of the national cochairs and I asked him to be an honorary cochair, he felt a deep sense of gratitude, but also pride, that all the years he had been working with me had come to fruition. He could feel like he was passing the baton in real time, that the organizing he had exposed me to, grounding communities across the country in nonviolence, had prepared me to create a space where I could bring those communities along.

GLORIA I would have been there no matter what, but soon I was asked by the younger women who were the march organizers to be an honorary chair—first with Harry Belafonte, then with Dolores Huerta, Angela Davis, and LaDonna Harris. The organizers multiplied my faith in the march because the group looked a lot like the country.

**Mia Ives-Rublee, Women's
March Disability Caucus Lead.**

CARMEN   We had spreadsheets of organizations, and multiple people tracking where we were in the relationship with that organization. Did they know about the march? Had they expressed interest in partnering? Is that partnership officially approved yet? Building relationships is a process that usually takes time, but we had only about five weeks until the march.

TONY CHOI
Deputy of Partnerships   There was so much butcher paper on the walls, notes everywhere. I don't think people understand the amount of work that was involved in selecting, vetting, and balancing voices. Carmen still had butcher paper on the walls from previous marches she'd organized. I said to myself, This woman is a movement woman!

BREANNE   As global partnerships grew, I didn't manage the time zones. I had no boundaries. It was actually really unhealthy. [*Laughs.*] I would be on the

Chicago

phone till like 2 A.M. talking to the West Coast, because most people were doing this before or after work.

   The phone would start ringing at like 6 A.M. on the East Coast. People would start working on the march, they'd skip their morning workout at the gym or whatever and spend their time working on this. And then after work they'd be working on this till 11, 12 at night, sometimes later. So I'd be on the phone till like 2 A.M. West Coast, but then by 4 A.M., my phone would be ringing with people in Europe, usually. And they're saying, "Good morning." They're all awake and they've had their coffee. But you know, there was no time. It was kind of like, I'll sleep later.

BOB   Designing merchandise, setting up our website and crowdfunding, and managing production were my favorite parts of organizing the march, because I was able to use my professional skills for such an important cause. For anyone coming into grassroots organizing work for the first time, I would highly recommend thinking about what your skills are already and how you can volunteer to help, instead of thinking you need to learn new skills or feeling like you don't have anything to offer.

VANESSA   I literally did not leave my computer. I worked up until 11:30 on New Year's Eve. And then I went out to the bar across the street to ring in the New Year. It was insane. The whole thing is a real blur.

LINDA   The majority of our outreach at that time was overcoming skepticism. The groups we reached out to as potential partners had heard all kinds of rumors, from the permit to lack of diversity, so it took a lot of work to get everyone on the same page, with a clear understanding of what the march was going to be about and how they could play a meaningful role in it.

CARMEN   We started sacrificing our families. My father is 92, and I didn't get to spend the holidays with him or my family. That was really hard. But the work was demanding—planning the day-of logistics, updating the state coordinators, seeing what needed to be done. My schedule ran from 7 A.M. to 1 A.M. I took the phone with me into the shower so I could be on conference calls.

SARAH SOPHIE   It was one thing after another. Once we got the permit, it was questions about safety, and it was this, that, and the other thing. The fact that women led the organizing of this march and have absolutely led the resistance, I don't think anyone can argue with that. A nation of women leaders has been created out of this election, and the ability to take women's leadership seriously, I feel like, is starting to sink in.

VANESSA   I held a 10:30 A.M. call every single day to coordinate. That was my life. I was the person who was supposed to be centralizing. I'm someone who's like, "Okay, we do this call and then we do this and then what's happening here?"

MRINALINI   It was a lot of chaos and phone calls and just figuring it out.

JANAYE We all collectively put together the pieces. Vanessa Wruble was the head of operations. And she was the one running the calls. A lot of times, it was me talking logistics, talking about the plan, talking about the various meetings that I was having with the National Park Service or with Metropolitan Police or with, you know, the mayor's office or whoever it was.

We had to work with the government agencies and their various processes, with the city of Washington, D.C., the federal government, and different agencies, each with its own structure and bureaucracy. I wish people understood a fraction of what it took to make this happen in a coordinated fashion. The press made such a big deal about permits in the early days, and then when I secured them, it was almost like it was a minor thing. To secure permits means you have to have every element of the plan in place. Bob says often, "If it wasn't for Janaye, we wouldn't have had a march." It is good to have that acknowledgment from her, but I do feel we alter history a bit when the herculean effort that so many people put into making the march a success goes unrecognized.

JENNA So we're sitting in the development meeting, and I'm thinking in my head, Holy shit, they are going to need to raise millions of dollars to pull this off in a classy, sophisticated way, just for bare-bones security, electronics, Wi-Fi, all that kind of stuff.

What I brought to the table, what I could foresee, was the world of people who don't ever show up at marches, who don't really care about activism, who were going to come to this thing. For instance, I have my activist friends and then I have my partying friends—you know how you roll in different circles. My party friends reached out to say, "Hey, we're getting a group of girls together to go down to the march, do you want to go?" And when these girls said that they were going to do a march, I knew in my bones that this was a very, very big thing. Because these girls don't show up really for anything.

MY MARCH

"MY YOUNGEST DAUGHTER'S POSTER READ 'MAKE MY FUTURE BETTER.'"

The morning after the election, there were swastikas drawn on the Hillary Clinton signs in our yard. My daughters, who are 9 and 12, were taunted in their school cafeteria for being Clinton supporters while the other kids chanted, "Lock her up! Lock her up!" One boy in my daughter's class told her that now that Trump had won, "We'll get rid of the sand ni**ers and the beaners, and the kikes will be next."

We're a Jewish, mixed-race family of transplants to the Deep South. My husband and I moved from New York City to our town right outside of St. Petersburg, Florida, when my mother retired here so we could take advantage of the babysitting. We've always felt like these tiny drops of blue in a giant red sea.

And this election felt particularly personal for me. I'm a black woman who was adopted and raised by a white family. Most of the men in my family are white New Yorkers who worked as policemen or firefighters, mostly in the Bronx. They saw daily what they would consider "the worst" aspects of minority culture, which colored their view of everything. Then my oldest brother, a fireman, died in 9/11. So I've experienced firsthand how Islamophobia and racism can affect how people think.

Before the march, we sat down with the girls and explained why we wanted to go and asked if they wanted to go with us. They're both very smart, very aware, and we don't hide much from them. They both wanted to attend, to have their voices heard. Then we asked if they had any ideas for posters. My youngest daughter's read: "Make my future better."

They expected about 5,000 people to show up for the march in St. Petersburg—there were 20,000. At the march, we realized that we in fact weren't tiny drops of blue—we were a giant blue wave. Since the march, my husband and daughters and I have gotten very involved in the resistance community here. My family has marched in the March for Science and the Climate March. I helped organize a Tax Day March in our little suburb. And even though this is the country of "Proud Deplorable" bumper stickers and Trump flags, we still had 1,000 people show up.

BETH WEINSTEIN
45, St. Petersburg, Florida, marketing director;
marched in Saint Petersburg, Florida

Alyssa Klein, Director of Social Media Strategy, at The Gathering for Justice offices in New York City.

"OUR VALUES AND OUR CHOICES WILL BE TESTED. . . . IN THE DAYS, WEEKS, MONTHS, AND YEARS TO COME . . . WE WILL NEED TO BECOME OUR OWN NORTH STAR."

**J. BOB ALOTTA,
EXECUTIVE DIRECTOR,
ASTRAEA LESBIAN FOUNDATION FOR JUSTICE**

ONSTAGE IN WASHINGTON, D.C.

WHAT MERYL SAID

Actress Uzo Aduba in
Washington, D.C., holding
a sign referring to actress
Meryl Streep's criticism of
Donald Trump.

DEC 29, 2016– JAN 9, 2017

ARTISTS AND ALLIES

THE LATE ARTIST AND ACTIVIST PAUL ROBESON SAID THAT "ARTISTS ARE THE GATEKEEPERS OF TRUTH. WE ARE CIVILIZATION'S RADICAL VOICE." INSPIRED BY THIS IDEA, THE WOMEN'S MARCH TEAM ORGANIZED AN ARTISTS' TABLE CHAIRED BY ACTRESS AMERICA FERRERA. THIS COLLABORATION RESULTED IN A LIST OF OVER 150 CELEBRITIES AND ARTISTS WHO PLEDGED TO SUPPORT THE MISSION OF THE WOMEN'S MARCH. THE INVOLVEMENT OF THESE ARTISTS HELPED ELEVATE THE MARCH IN PUBLIC CONVERSATION AND IN SOME CASES INSPIRED FANS TO TRAVEL TO WASHINGTON TO MARCH ALONGSIDE THEM.

CARMEN   Early on, we began working with America Ferrera on the Artists' Table. I brought in some of the elders from past movements. Gloria Steinem sat with all of us and talked about her involvement in the feminist movement. Mr. Belafonte came and shared an account of his time during the civil rights movement and talked about his experience with Dr. King in the original March on Washington.

PAOLA   Having artists involved in the resistance to amplify and uplift those stories was a crucial part of our strategy. We need to change the hearts of folks, and to reinspire people to keep them engaged. And you do that with art and with love. I get asked a lot, "How are you going to resist for four years? Isn't it going to be exhausting?" And at first that question really bothered me, because I didn't know the answer. Because it is exhausting to be fighting, to be in constant resistance.

And I remember I was in the car going down to D.C. and reading an article, and they asked this other woman the same thing. She talked about how angry she was, and how that was the thing that was feeding her and her resistance. And I realized that that was not going to work. For her or for me. At that moment I had my own personal realization, which we've heard from every major activist and revolutionary thinker on this planet: that what it comes down to at the end of the day is love. We must resist out of a place of love—not anger, not revenge, not fear, but out of love for our communities, love for our democracy, love for our freedom.

The week before Christmas we were working 15-hour days. We were honored to call Mr. Belafonte's office our headquarters. One night, to my delight, I had two wonderful visitors come to our office. The first was my three-year-old son Mateo Ali. I hadn't been home much so he came to pay me a visit, even though he should have been sleeping. The second was Mr. Belafonte himself, and an hour later I was sitting at his desk with Mateo Ali on my lap. Mr. B (as we affectionately call him) reminisced that night about organizing the March on Washington. And he said something else to me that I will never forget: "When the movement is strong, the music is strong." This is a man who knew of what he spoke. He had organized the entire artist

> ## "WE'RE MARCHING BECAUSE THE MOST POWERFUL MAN IN THE WORLD SAYS IT'S OK TO SEXUALLY ASSAULT WOMEN . . . AND WE SAY NO WAY."
>
> **YVETTE COOPER, LABOUR MEMBER OF PARLIAMENT**
>
> **ONSTAGE IN LONDON**

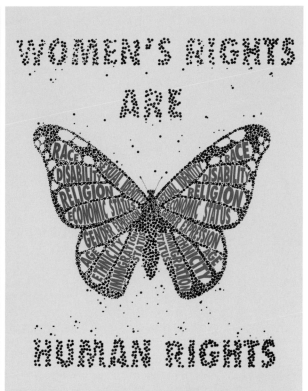

Previous page: Amplifier artwork from (clockwise from top left) Brooke Fischer, Alexandría Lee, Mari Mansfield, Dawline-Jane Oni-Eseleh. Opposite: Jessica Sabogal's work for Amplifier.

community for the 1963 March on Washington—Mahalia Jackson, Bob Dylan, Sidney Poitier, Joan Baez, and so many others who came to the march because Mr. B had brought them there. I knew this was exactly what we had to do. Our movement was strong, and now we needed to make our music strong.

SARAH SOPHIE We held Artists' Table dinners at my house, which ended up being so fruitful. At one of them, fashion designers including Mara Hoffman and Rachel Comey birthed the idea of a weekend online sale in support of the march. In the same meeting filmmakers began the process of creating a "Why We March" video as well as a video on Kingian principles of nonviolence. Alyssa Klein and I started calls for art online as well as calls for "Why I March" crowdsourced videos. The creative resistance was born on these nights and has continued to be a huge force.

ALYSSA KLEIN, Director of Social Media Strategy and National Organizer Artists were really the people who allowed us to spread the word about the march and our intersectional messaging beyond the initial group that followed the Women's March after November 9. It was incredible to see artists so selflessly drop everything and do what they could to help us get the word out. No one was doing it for personal gain—people truly wanted to use their platform for the public good. Above all, sharing artwork on Instagram was one of the best and most impactful ways we spread the word. Another cool thing was that artists and celebrities used their platforms to elevate the work of young-women-of-color artists.

GINNY We put out feelers for musicians. Toshi Reagon was actually the very first to come on board as the musical director. She comes from an activist background; her mother, the singer Bernice Johnson Reagon, founded Sweet Honey in the Rock and had been active in the civil rights movement. And then we said we needed to build a show. So let's make a wish list and just put the feelers out to some artists and see who's interested in being part of this thing that we're calling the Women's March. At that point, we had no budget.

MY MARCH

"MY OWN DAUGHTERS TAUGHT ME ABOUT WOMEN'S RIGHTS."

Aparna, my daughter, found out about the Kolkata Women's March, so we went to the park to join. There were about twenty other people there—many were American students. There was one American lady who has lived in Kolkata a long time. She was married to an Indian gentleman. There were two other Indian ladies who marched with us and who were making the banners. We started making them too. My banner said "Women's Rights." We were singing in Bengali too, saying that women should have women's rights. We said some things about Trump also. Ha. Trump. How people voted for him I don't know.

I consider myself a feminist, but my daughter is even more of one because she grew up in America. I grew up in India, and I got married here. So I wasn't exposed to the same things. When I was young, my sisters and I went to an all-girls school. My parents have no sons, so I wasn't immediately aware of the differences in how boys and girls are raised. But my aunt had a son and a daughter and raised them differently. Even in the U.S., some Indian people have daughters and sons and raise them differently. The son goes to private school and the daughter goes to public school. They say, "The son needs more education and a good job. But my daughter will marry and will go to a local college."

My own daughters taught me about women's rights while they were growing up, and now they are very much involved in politics. My younger daughter was pregnant and marching in Washington when I was marching in Kolkata. It was the only time I have ever marched for anything—and that day the march was all over the world. It was my privilege to join. I was proud of my daughters and proud that I was included.

MAITREYEE MUKHERJEE
67, Kolkata, India, retired; marched in Kolkata

HEAR OUR VOICE
women's rights are human rights

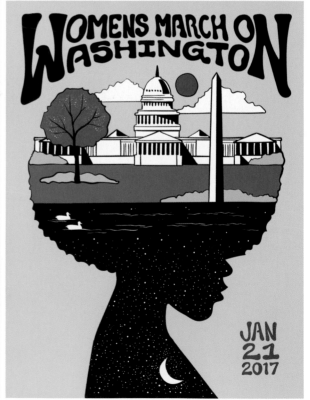

TOSHI REAGON
Music Director

When I got a call from Ginny to join the team, I was surprised. A lot of people would have been happy to have speakers and a DJ and occasionally someone really, really famous, but Ginny insisted that music would hold the dominant space onstage in D.C. She said, "It needs to be a band and I think Toshi should do this. She's been doing this for years."

GINNY

As you would expect, the lion's share of people we reached out to in the very early stages were unresponsive. Working on the management side with musicians, I know they constantly get hit up to do free work for amazing nonprofits. I mean, every major artist you know could spend all of their time just doing free shows. But they need to make a living too.

We also reached out to African singer-songwriter and activist Angélique Kidjo, who's been a friend of mine for many years. And Angélique immediately committed to the cause, not because it was already a big, giant buzzy thing or because it was going to help promote her career, but because she believed in it. She is the kind of artist I love working with. And to me it was no surprise. When I look at the people who are always showing up when showing up needs to happen, it's often African women.

TOSHI

Ginny is really smart, with a beautiful heart. And because she's worked with music and bands and worked inside these machines where you have to gather 40,000 to 50,000 people, she visualized the stage as a central place for gathering.

PAOLA

In the end we had more than 150 artists sign on to the Artists' Table in support of the Women's March. They supported us with their physical presence and also with their social media presence. We were sure to tell them: "This is not the Oscars, it's a march, so you need to come prepared to march."

Along with the music, we had Amplifier. They came to me and said they wanted to curate art for us. All of the artwork that has been so emblematic and that has come to be associated with the Women's March comes from Amplifier. It lived online and it was downloadable completely for free, which was part of the reason for its success.

Cleo Barnett, Amplifier's program director, and I worked very closely together on choosing the images. Part of my job was curating the visual story that was being told around the march in images. What kind of visual messaging were we putting out to the public? The images that we chose were very specific around the communities that we were trying to protect. It was all very intentional.

Opposite: Amplifier artwork from (clockwise from top left) Liza Donovan, Kafesha Thomas, Kelley Wills, and Katie Rita.

¡SÍ SE PUEDE!

Los Angeles

BY JOSE ANTONIO VARGAS

HOW TO BE AN ALLY

Jose Antonio Vargas, a journalist and filmmaker, is the founder and chief executive officer of the nonprofit media and culture organization Define American.

The email landed in my inbox the Monday after Thanksgiving, some 20 days after Donald Trump was elected president. "Women's March," the subject line read. Paola Mendoza, one of my best friends and one of the march organizers, wrote: "I want to throw your hat into the ring for a speaking slot. Are you down for that? I want to make sure that's not poking the lion too much."

"Poking the lion" is one way to describe what I've been doing for the past few years. Against the advice of immigration lawyers, I was "poking the lion" by disclosing my undocumented immigrant status in an essay in *The New York Times Magazine* in 2011. Three years later, with Paola at my side in Texas, just a few miles from the U.S.-Mexico border, I was "poking the lion" by deciding to risk getting arrested by boarding a domestic flight. (For undocumented immigrants, traveling without proper identification is risky, even within the borders of the United States.)

By living a very public life as "the most famous illegal in America," as Bill O'Reilly once called me, everyday life can feel like "poking the lion." Nevertheless, my goal in coming out as undocumented is to let people in, to share the realities and the challenges of living and surviving as an American without papers. I am also hoping that sharing my personal story will prompt other people to share theirs, not only undocumented immigrants themselves but allies of undocumented people: our classmates and coworkers, our neighbors and friends. If all of the estimated 11 million undocumented immigrants in the U.S. have at least three distinct allies in their lives, then we're conservatively talking about an issue that directly impacts some 44 million people.

The uncomfortable but necessary truth is there are no movements without allies. Allyship forces you to look outside of yourself, to claim your rightful place with dignity while realizing that you're not the only person in the room. You never are. You never will be. In the past few years I've learned that to attract allies, you must also be willing to become an ally. So the moment Paola asked me if I was interested in a speaking slot, my gut reaction was no—no, thank you. To me, being an ally to the movement for women's rights and gender equality means knowing when and how to step back, listen, and learn. Being a male feminist means putting women first in a society that rarely does.

The moment I said no, I thought of the role that immigrant women of all ages—documented and undocumented, from various racial, ethnic, and economic backgrounds—play in the national and global struggle for immigrant rights. Women, in fact, carry the immigrant rights movement on their individual and collective backs, insisting that we face the many facets of the issue. Immigration is a racial justice issue. Immigration is an economic justice issue. Immigration is an environmental justice issue. Immigration is an LGBTQ issue. Immigration is a women's rights issue. Immigration has been and will always be about families, with immigrant women front and center. Yet too often, in the way the news media frames immigration, in the way movies, television shows, and popular culture portray the issue, in the way politicians use immigrants as pawns—in

ARGUABLY THE MOST INCLUSIVE GATHERING FOR IMMIGRANT RIGHTS THAT I HAVE EVER WITNESSED WAS AT THE WOMEN'S MARCH.

the way Trump ran the most anti-immigrant campaign in modern presidential history while Melania Trump, an immigrant First Lady, looked on—the voices, faces, and stories of immigrant women are marginalized and sidelined, segregated and simplified and sanitized, if not altogether ignored.

Not this time. Not at the Women's March. Not during the largest single-day protest in U.S. history.

Looking back at it now, it's stunning to remember that arguably the most inclusive gathering for immigrant rights that I have ever witnessed was at the Women's March. Instead of taking a speaking slot in Washington, D.C., I supported my friends who organized the march, among them Paola. I spent most of the day backstage, passing around water bottles, escorting this or that speaker, guiding this or that VIP. I marveled at the kaleidoscope of women who took the stage. The actress and activist America Ferrera, a stalwart champion for immigrant rights, began the morning by declaring: "We will not go from being a nation of immigrants to a nation of ignorance." The march's youngest speaker, six-year-old Sophie Cruz, was surrounded by her undocumented parents, Zoyla and Raul, as she said, in English and then in Spanish: "Let us fight with love, faith, and courage so that our families will not be destroyed." And of course the singular Angela Davis, a constant conscience of our country, connected the dots: "This is a country anchored in slavery and colonialism, which means for better or for worse the very history of the United States is a history of immigration and enslavement." Davis ended her remarks by saying there would be "resistance on the ground, resistance in the classrooms, resistance on the job, resistance in our art and in our music."

Women, as ever, will lead the resistance, and men must be their allies.

Dr. Tamara Lee,
volunteer organizer
in Washington, D.C.

AIN'T I A WOMAN?

'S NONE
SINESS!

DARING DISCUSSIONS

ORGANIZING IS COMPLICATED. THERE ARE DIFFERING APPROACHES TO CHANGE, AND CONFLICTS RELATED TO RACE, ECONOMIC STATUS, IMMIGRATION STATUS, ABILITY, RELIGION, AND GENDER-RELATED PRIVILEGE. FROM THE BEGINNING, WOMEN'S MARCH ORGANIZERS PLEDGED TO CONFRONT THESE ISSUES, NOT HIDE THEM. INSPIRED BY THE GATHERING FOR JUSTICE'S ADHERENCE TO MARTIN LUTHER KING'S ORGANIZING PRINCIPLES OF NON-VIOLENCE, THEY ENGAGED IN DISCUSSIONS BY GROUNDING THEMSELVES IN LOVE AND TRYING TO SUSPEND JUDGMENT ABOUT OTHERS.

CARMEN As we were gathering supporters for the Women's March, we needed to create a transparent process so that everyone could engage and really look at their issues. We began having what we now call "daring discussions" with the white women in the space. Even though people were talking about centering women of color, a lot of us organizers who were leaders and women of color had a very challenging time. I felt angry, I felt used. I felt, Why should I constantly build bridges when at the end of the day people are gonna vote in their own self-interest rather than for marginalized communities? But I've been trained to come from a place of suspending judgment. And in that spirit, I thought it was my responsibility to be there and be part of the organizing.

LINDA I'm a walking daring discussion. I'm a Muslim woman from a directly impacted community. I am Palestinian American. I'm an outspoken activist and a Brooklynite who is a little rough around the edges. For some women within the Women's March, speaking with me was the first meaningful conversation they'd had with a Muslim woman or a Palestinian, and my approach of directly speaking the truth isn't always comfortable. I truly believe in people wearing their principles on their sleeve, and there were many conversations that needed to happen to understand where everyone came from and why they were here now. We had to listen to women tell us how upset they were that their family voted for Trump, not knowing how triggered that made women of color feel. I learned that we couldn't shy away from hard conversations. We must stay at the table. We must struggle through this.

CARMEN We talked a lot about being high-impact and low-ego. In other words, there's a lane for everyone, keep your eyes on the prize, and focus on getting the work done; all contributions are valuable. And also, when you feel mad, ask yourself: Is this really about me? Or is it possibly about something else?

TOSHI The big meetings were kind of chaotic. Ideas were thrown around quickly and you didn't get to meet everybody. It was an intense atmosphere and there wasn't a lot of time for feelings. When people are used to having a dominant voice, they often need to learn how to share. Sometimes that happened and sometimes people held their tongue and moved past a hard moment. I witnessed all of that happening.

CASSADY We established the voice and the tone of the Women's March very, very early on. I don't take credit for it. I had been working with Tamika and Linda and Carmen for a number of years, helping with communications. We were inheriting a situation where the only people involved at that point had been white women—and they had called it the Million Woman March. And so, it was already a shit show. [*Laughs.*]

So we had to, first of all, come up with an organizing agreement. And that was that we will always have these daring discussions. With these kinds of confrontational but still loving conversations, we would hold our organizing collective accountable. Many white women wanted to talk

Gloria Steinem shares her march insights with Paola Mendoza.

"SOMETIMES WE MUST PUT OUR BODIES WHERE OUR BELIEFS ARE. SOMETIMES PRESSING SEND IS NOT ENOUGH."

**GLORIA STEINEM,
WOMEN'S MARCH HONORARY COCHAIR**

ONSTAGE IN WASHINGTON, D.C.

about "unity," but without acknowledging our privilege; that erodes trust and then it all falls apart.

PAOLA Women of color had to learn to trust white women, because we felt stabbed in the back by the white community. Our communities are under attack because their demographic had voted for Trump.

So there was definitely—*animosity* is too strong of a word, but there was definitely *mistrust*. There was a prove-yourself-to-me mentality: Prove to me that you are not going to throw me under the bus when the time comes. We had to have these daring discussions, because they were a reflection of what needed to happen in the country.

SARAH SOPHIE Daring discussions were often uncomfortable. We had come from being divided within our own party and within our own progressive

---

MY MARCH

"I COULD NOT SEE MY CHILD MARGINALIZED."

After a few years of being unhappy and generally frustrated, my 10-year-old child came out to me by telling me that he wanted to be "known as a boy."

I will never forget that night. It was the evening of July 28, 2016, and we were watching the Democratic National Convention. Sarah McBride, the national press secretary of the Human Rights Campaign, introduced herself as "a proud transgender American." Moved by her speech, I said to my child, "You can be anything you want to be. This is the first openly transgender person to speak at a national convention. We have a black president, and we are going to have a female president" (so I thought). Within 20 minutes the child I had thought was a girl told me what had been on his mind since he was five years old: that he was really a boy. I knew instantly that this was the missing piece to my child's happiness. We supported him and spent the next few months paving the way for him. Once the election was over, I felt I had no choice but to ramp up my political advocacy.

I've been moderately active in the past, participating in lobbying events and rallies, but I wasn't sure if I wanted to attend the march at first. I worried about the huge crowd and possible violence. However, it became clear to me, especially with the new administration, which seems determined to marginalize people like my child, that I could not stand by. I have always considered myself a fighter for civil and social rights, but I felt more woke than ever because of my recent involvement with the LGBTQ community. I could not see my child marginalized. I wiggled out of my comfort zone and made the commitment to go.

My sister flew in from California, my niece from Missouri, and my friend and her college-age daughter

came from North Carolina. A few of my local friends joined us. My house was full of women eager to have our voices heard and numbers counted. We walked to the Metro early in the morning and found it packed. It took us almost 45 minutes just to get out of the station. I have never seen anything like it in my 20 years in D.C. Even though we were all smashed together, everyone was smiling and talking—nothing like the typical pushing and surliness.

I was so happy to see representatives from the organizations supporting the LGBTQ community—it made me feel like part of a bigger community and gave me hope that there were so many people outside of my D.C. "bubble" fighting for the rights of marginalized people. We truly felt like we had a common bond that day. And my child's rights are on the line. I want my kids to know that we cannot just sit and let things happen to us—we must fight for the things we want in life. My kids are so proud of my marching, and we look at the pictures often. We care about science, we care about immigrants, we care about LGBTQ rights, we care about people of color. I am proud that they are allies and good-hearted preteens who know the difference between hate and love.

Every parent loves their child and will do anything to protect them. In my case, I happen to have a transgender child. I know that he is happier and healthier living as the gender he identifies with. To take his rights away in the bathroom, classroom, or workforce would be removing him from society. That I will not accept. For that I marched and will continue to march.

SARAH WATSON
52, Washington, D.C., stay-at-home mom; marched in Washington.

Women's March cochair
Carmen Perez at The Gathering for
Justice offices in New York City.

Social Media

COMMS

The team reacts to a report that attendance forecasted for Washington, D.C., has surged.

movement. A week after the election, we had people from the Clinton campaign, people from the Sanders camp, and people who I still don't even know who they voted for working together pretty harmoniously and grappling with the difficult issues.

LINDA   Half of us had worked on the Hillary campaign. And the rest of us were Bernie. If I could be a national surrogate for Bernie Sanders and help organize the largest single-day protest after a horrific election with people who worked on the Hillary campaign, then I tell people

Washington, D.C.

all the time, "Stop with that Hillary/Bernie shit. We already proved that these two groups can work together. We were always on the same side."

MARIAM EHRARI
Deputy of Operations and National Organizer

To me, there is no doubt that the Women's March was sparked because of the fact that the most qualified candidate in history to ever run for the presidency, who also happened to be the first woman to secure a major-party nomination, lost because we are still living in a sexist society. The way I saw it, the left just egregiously lost an election because we couldn't get our act together and were too busy pointing fingers internally, being baited by bullshit conversations about Hillary's emails. So we needed to take the loss of this election as a lesson and come together to make sure this doesn't happen again. So I sucked up the hurt and anger and agreed to work with some of the people who had made my life and the lives of my colleagues on the campaign more difficult, under the assumption that we were coming together for the greater good. There were definitely difficult moments around this topic—some addressed and some left unaddressed—during the planning of the march and, I'll be honest, it's still a work in progress to this day. But I think it's more important than ever to work through challenges like this one. Because if we can't do it, how do we expect the rest of America to do it?

DE'ARA

I was still mourning, for the country and for Hillary. Literally 10 years of my life were dedicated to getting this woman elected. And my grandmother had passed away during the campaign. So after the election, I was dealing with all of these things that I really hadn't dealt with. And I wanted to show Tamika, Linda, Bob, and the rest of those women what I had learned from Hillary about leadership and collaboration. It started with listening, then asking the question "How can I help?" and ended with getting it done, whatever the "it" was. No ego, no drama, just a selflessness that comes when women work together.

I thought, I'm going to bring Hillary into this space through how I treat these women. I remember one of my first conversations with Linda—was it Linda? Or maybe it was Carmen. It was about partnership, and I said, "Oh, I'll call this person, call that person. I'll do this, I'll do that." And she was kind of like, "Well, what do you want out of it?" And I said, "What? Girl? What are you talking about? This is what we do. This is how we roll. I'm giving of myself, my labor and connections, and I'm not out for personal gain."

MEREDITH

One of the things that I am most proud of is how well I navigated the aftermath of the election. I never said anything negative about Bernie Sanders or Bernie Sanders people. I was proud that all the Hillary people who were involved and who had key roles could show that they were not poor losers and that they were about the greater good and the values that we had always been for.

"A MAN WON THE WHITE HOUSE WITH ANGER AND HATE AND OUR KIDS WATCHED IT HAPPEN. NOW IT'S OUR JOB TO LET THEM WATCH US FIGHT BACK."

HAWAII STATE REPRESENTATIVE BETH FUKUMOTO

ONSTAGE IN HONOLULU

SOPHIE ELLMAN-GOLAN, Deputy of Social Media and National Organizer One thing that feels incredibly special about Women's March, and a reason why I am still incredibly proud to be part of this team, is that since the inception of the march, we have been having the hard conversations that no one wants to have. We're first having them internally, and then we're having them publicly once we have sort of figured out how to articulate the issues to ourselves and to each other. And that's a result of the deep love that we all have for each other in doing this work.

Do we sometimes drive each other up the wall? Of course, like anyone's sisters and coworkers will do sometimes. But we've created a space where I, as a Jewish woman, can sit down with Tamika and say, "Let's really talk about antiblackness in Jewish communities, and let's talk about anti-Semitism in black communities." That sums up for me what the Women's March is about—agreeing to be brave together.

PAOLA So yes, there were tears, and yes, voices were raised at times. But at the end of the day, if we were coming from a place of love, and if we were very clear about where we wanted to go, then those daring discussions didn't destroy us, they actually made us stronger.

SOPHIE We didn't know it at the time, but seven months after the march, our country would end up in the throes of a daring discussion because of the white supremacist protest in Charlottesville. How do we allow that daring discussion to make us stronger? There is no easy way around that. It's going to be hard. The hope is that it is going to make us a better country. A large chunk of my responsibilities leading up to and following the march involved posting on social media. Daring discussions helped inspire me to push the envelope, to introduce our vast audience to ideas they hadn't considered before, to encourage white women in particular to confront white supremacy. While we are not a white organization by any means, we are seen that way, and that, in my mind, made us a more palatable voice for radical statements.

New York City

BOB   At the outset of my work on the march, I'll be honest and admit that terms like "intersectional," "white privilege," and "racial justice" were sadly not part of my daily lexicon. But they should have been. We all must start on the path from where we are. When Tamika started explaining why we must center Black Lives Matter and criminal justice reform in our Women's March platform, my life forever changed. Looking back, I can see that the systems of oppression and white supremacy in this country depend on people like me remaining ignorant. Since November 9, I have been learning and opening my eyes wider every day. And for those of us who are new to this movement work, we must commit to staying awake, no matter how hard or painful it may be.

ALYSSA   One day ShiShi Rose, a black writer and activist on the Women's March's social media team, came to me because she felt that we were letting people off the hook too much and that we weren't being brave about challenging all the white women following us to acknowledge their privilege and to better understand the roots of racism and white supremacy, among other things. ShiShi wrote an Instagram post introducing herself to our followers and speaking out about this. A lot of white women who were following us responded negatively.

There were some good responses, but there was also a lot of pushback. So we ended up doing a Facebook Live video with ShiShi and Cassady [who is white]. Cassady spoke about what it means to be an ally. ShiShi shared her experiences as a black woman. The discussion was very divisive. A lot of white middle-aged women felt threatened by ShiShi's comments. But it was one of the best things we ever did, because we started this conversation.

CASSADY   All I did was get on Facebook Live and agree with and reflect everything that ShiShi was saying, and for some people that made the difference between them reacting defensively versus hearing the intent of the message. It's ridiculous, but that's exactly how white supremacy works.

SOPHIE   What I didn't realize, what I never considered (there's white privilege in a nutshell), was that any backlash we receive lands hardest on Linda, Tamika, and Carmen, the three most visible women of color at the helm of Women's March. This happened when I, as Women's March, posted a message wishing a happy birthday to Assata Shakur [a former Black Liberation Army member whose conviction for the murder of a state trooper has been widely contested]. Who was blamed for that? Linda. This also happened when we, as an organization, decided to take on the NRA by organizing a march called NRA2DOJ. Who did the NRA personally come after? Linda, Tamika, and Carmen.

There is safety in anonymity. But it was only ever my safety, as a relatively unknown white woman behind the Women's March's avatar. For high-profile women of color, there is no safety, no anonymity.

MRINALINI   We disagree with each other, we have arguments, but at the end of the day there is no question that we are part of a movement family. I just hope that we can keep building on the network that we have so that the local chapters also learn and build that level of trust within their local community. Because this is how the movement is going to last and how it's going to be truly effective—when our Unity Principles are truly being practiced in the work that we are doing.

JAN 12, 2017

WHY WE MARCH: THE UNITY PRINCIPLES

AS THE DIVERSE LIST OF PARTNERS EXPANDED, THE ORGANIZERS NEEDED TO CLARIFY THE GOALS OF THE MARCH. THEY UNVEILED THEIR POLICY PLATFORM, FOUR WEEKS IN THE MAKING. CALLED THE UNITY PRINCIPLES, THE PLATFORM WAS ROOTED IN THE IDEA THAT "MY LIBERATION IS BOUND IN YOURS," A PHRASE MADE POPULAR BY ABORIGINAL ACTIVIST LILLA WATSON. IT WAS SHAPED BY INPUT FROM MORE THAN 20 LEADERS FROM VARIOUS MOVEMENTS. THERE ARE EIGHT UNITY PRINCIPLES: ENDING VIOLENCE, REPRODUCTIVE RIGHTS, LGBTQIA RIGHTS, WORKERS' RIGHTS, CIVIL RIGHTS, DISABILITY RIGHTS, IMMIGRANT RIGHTS, AND ENVIRONMENTAL JUSTICE.

Stick with love. Hate is too great a burden to bear!

— Martin Luther King

BLM!

GAY & Proud!!!

Women's Rights!

Ventura, California

LINDA The Unity Principles reflect the participation of women of color. We were very clear that racial justice, maternal justice, issues of immigration, reproductive freedom, civil liberties, voting rights—we made sure issues impacting all women, but in particular women of color, were central to our Unity Principles. I don't know if that would have happened without women of color participating. Especially at the highest levels of leadership.

CASSADY With the Unity Principles, we wanted to remind people of what we really believe our country is about, what our values really are. We needed to reaffirm them. We wanted them to reflect what we were for rather than talking about what we're against.

CARMEN The principles needed to be rooted in the world we wanted to create for women and our communities. Women are not a monolith, and so we needed to bring our full selves. Meaning I am a Chicana, from immigrant parents, with family members who are incarcerated.

We knew indigenous women had to be involved, because their voices have been consistently erased from the historical and political narrative. And ultimately they established a collective called Indigenous Women Rise and mobilized 1,000 indigenous women to come to Washington, D.C.

"PREJUDICE NEVER HAS AND NEVER WILL SET THE PEOPLE FREE."

ASHLEY HARRINGTON, BLACK LIVES MATTER

ONSTAGE IN CINCINNATI, OHIO

JANET MOCK, Activist, Writer, and Women's March Speaker I helped shape the Unity Principles with other activists across the country, but many people were concentrating on siloed stuff.

VANESSA We had a bunch of people who hopefully believed in the same thing but who were vastly different from one another in every way, shape, and form. And we were trying to put a message out into the world that would change the world, in two and a half months. Yeah. Shit got messy. Yes. Yes, it did.

SARAH SOPHIE When we put out the Unity Principles, they were really embraced pretty wholeheartedly. But the critique we got the most was about the message being "scattered" or "unfocused." Or people would ask, "Why are there so many issues?" They asked this because they wanted it to feel easy. But the Unity Principles reflect *all* women and all their intersecting identities, which historically feminism has left out.

Washington, D.C.

JANET   I noticed some gaps when I saw the initial document. There was no mention of HIV/AIDS, which is something that black communities, black women, and queer folk are still struggling with. There was also no mention of sex workers, which was vital to me.

SOPHIE   There have been long-term, intergenerational debates in the feminist movement about sex workers. Some people think sex work is only oppressive and that sex workers have no agency. But plenty of sex workers choose the job, and the criminalization of sex work puts them in more danger, not less. Janet Mock made sure that sex workers' rights were represented in the Unity Principles. It was such a huge moment to see sex workers' rights included in a mainstream feminist manifesto, and when the line temporarily disappeared from the Unity Principles— for a couple of hours—it was seen as such a betrayal. We were getting dragged on Twitter about it—rightly so. When we put the line back in, we upgraded it from "we stand in solidarity with the sex workers' rights movement" to "we stand in *full* solidarity." And I know we lost a lot of trust in the sex worker community because of it, trust we have an obligation to earn back. We connected with people who have written very public critiques and said, "You're totally right, let's do this better."

JANET   It's great that we have the gender-inclusive language and trans-inclusive language, but what are the issues beyond someone's getting killed or someone's not being allowed to use the restroom? Knowing that a lot of low-income trans folk engage in underground economies like the drug trade and sex work, I felt that we needed to mention that. It should not just be a trans thing, it should be under labor. We needed to acknowledge that this labor too matters. And though we may not do it ourselves, may not make those same choices, we should not judge someone for making the choices that they feel that they need to make for their own survival.

TED JACKSON
Women's March Logistics
Team Accessibility Lead and
National Organizer   There was also a point in time where the Unity Principles had gotten released but the language wasn't fully inclusive of disability. And I remember having a conversation with Mia [Ives-Rublee] about what we should do. Folks reached out to me, and I think I connected them to Linda Sarsour at the time, and to Mia and other folks.

MIA IVES-RUBLEE
Women's March Disability
Caucus Lead and
National Organizer   The disability issue was actually quite a bit of a struggle. I created a Facebook account that was called the Women's March on Washington Disability Caucus. And I started contacting leaders within the disability community to try and help build our own platform that we could eventually just send up to the national organizers so that they could include it in their principles. It took about two weeks, I think. And we created this document, which we posted online and we sent to the national organizers. They eventually incorporated it into the Unity Principles.

SOPHIE   Today, if I could change something in the Unity Principles, I would have included Jewish women—they aren't mentioned specifically, which I

Washington, D.C.

think was a mistake and something I should have caught and flagged. I think a lot has shifted in the past seven or eight months in terms of the need to recognize Jews as a marginalized group. I think that that shift is really visible and now we're starting to address that more, particularly after Charlottesville.

MRINALINI We all have a certain level of privilege that we are entering movement work with. I see it as my job to harness whatever privilege I do have and use that to do good. I hear a lot of folks asking, "Well, what is my voice going to do? Or what is my contribution going to be? I'm already so targeted, why do I have to open myself up to even more targeting?" I'm like, I hear you, but when activism is led by the most impacted people, that is when it is the strongest. I wholeheartedly believe that.

It doesn't matter how afraid I am; my voice needs to be in the Unity Principles and my face needs to be up on the website to let people see that everybody is a part of this fight. If that inspires even 10 more people to believe that they can do this too, that's what is needed.

Rowan Blanchard at the
Women's March in Los Angeles.

BY ROWAN
BLANCHARD

AN OPEN LETTER TO GROWN-UPS

Rowan Blanchard is an
activist and actress who
starred in the Disney Channel
series *Girl Meets World*.

I was asked to speak at the Women's March in L.A., and of course I said yes. I try to take any opportunity I can to be a representative for my generation (I was 15 at the time of the march), especially because during and after the election I think people forgot that there were a lot of us who had worked hard to get our parents, families, or friends to vote, even though we couldn't vote ourselves. There was this weird feeling of being left behind in a lot of conversations. I wanted to make it clear that teenagers deserve a seat at the table. I wanted to talk about my generation because I feel like often when we are talked about, it's not from our mouths but from adults who are writing *about* us.

I get asked a lot: "Why are you involved in politics? You're so young, don't you want to enjoy being a kid?" I really don't understand that thought process. Let's say you're a teen who is an undocumented immigrant. Is someone going to ask you why you are involved in politics? And then you get deported? The idea that teens shouldn't be interested in politics just doesn't make sense to me. Even though we can't vote yet, we young people are all so, so affected by this presidency. And we're incredibly aware of it.

My generation isn't sheltered like previous generations of teens have been. The presidential race acted as an age equalizer. We all have access to the same information because we are all on the Internet, and we are working hard to educate one another. I learned not just about feminism but about *intersectional* feminism from other teenagers, so I felt it was only fair to acknowledge teenagers at the Women's March. Teenagers on the Internet explained to me what *queer* meant, what the word *biracial* really meant. I am incredibly impressed with how my generation takes the time to educate one another. When the Black Lives Matter movement started, I, coming from a place of white privilege, needed to better understand its motives. And other teens explained it to me without softening it—and in a more inclusive, straightforward, just-the-facts way that, to be frank, I didn't learn in middle school history class. Now I take history classes and think, This isn't all that happened! This isn't the whole truth! I wouldn't know if it weren't for other teenagers breaking down the information for me on the Internet.

I will not be old enough to vote in the midterm elections. But I'll still be working my ass off to get people who are 18 to vote. So if you want to have an influence, you need to include us! If young people get discouraged and decide it's not worth voting, we're going to be stuck in a Republican mess for God knows how long.

When I wrote my speech for the march, I couldn't just say about the future: "It's OK; we'll be fine." Instead, to teens I say: Reach out. You've got to have your "witch crew," your people you can text and check in on. When I've felt myself losing hope, it's other girls and queer young people who have kept me going. When someone checks in on me, I'm grateful, and when I check in on a friend who is a lot more affected by what's going on than I am, I know we're supporting each other. We have to have our own network of healing.

SPEAKING AT THE MARCH WAS A WAY FOR ME TO REMIND PEOPLE OF ALL AGES THAT IF YOU LOSE TEENAGERS, YOU LOSE THE NEXT VOTING GENERATION.

Speaking at the march was a way for me to remind people of all ages that if you lose teenagers, you lose the next voting generation. We saw that a lot of people didn't vote in this election because they didn't think their one vote would make a difference. People genuinely believe that. That's my biggest concern. Young people are taught to believe what adults tell us, and when you act like your vote doesn't matter, that's the message we get. I was lucky to grow up in a household where I was allowed to question adults and engage in conversations about what I believe and learn from them. But for the vast majority of teens, that doesn't exist—especially if you are growing up in a household that is racist or homophobic. So my biggest plea is to adults: Include us in your conversations. Give us more platforms, and don't talk down to us when you do include us. Our voices matter.

DEC 31, 2016– JAN 21, 2017

OPERATION HEADCOUNT

AS THE POPULARITY OF THE MARCH SNOWBALLED IN THE SOCIAL-MEDIA SPHERE, THE ORGANIZERS STRUGGLED TO UNDERSTAND HOW MANY PEOPLE WERE ACTUALLY COMING TO MARCH IN D.C., AND FROM WHERE.

"SISTERS AND BROTHERS, YOU ARE WHAT DEMOCRACY LOOKS LIKE."

LINDA SARSOUR,
WOMEN'S MARCH COCHAIR

ONSTAGE IN WASHINGTON, D.C.

MAKE AMERICA SMART AGAIN

LOVE NOT HATE MAKES AMERICA GREAT!

Los Angeles

OPERATION HEADCOUNT

MRINALINI   By mid-December, we were expecting over 200,000 people coming to the march, but because of the nature of how the march planning had started (on Facebook!), we had no centralized database to measure attendance. Operation Headcount was the solution! It was the brainchild of Sam Frank, our tech guy, and me; his sister Tina Frank helped us out as well, and we were supported by Vanessa Wruble, Jenna Arnold, and dozens of volunteers.

JENNA   At one point the Washington police department was like, You guys have got to get your hands around the number of people who are truly coming. And so we launched Operation Headcount on a Google form.

JANAYE   Leading up to the march, we consistently kept the number at 200,000. We did this in part because we didn't have a firm mechanism to count all of the people who said they were coming. We had created Operation Headcount to track numbers, but not everyone who intended to come to the march responded. Finally, Sam Frank helped analyze our numbers based on an algorithm that he developed. When we had our final meeting with the collective agencies, including the National Park Service, Sam told me that he thought we would have a half million people, and I communicated that to the agencies.

EMMA   About five weeks into the planning, Mrinalini and I had a phone call where we realized the largest number of buses in the history of history were about to embark for D.C., and no one knew where they would park.

MRINALINI   There were two parts to Operation Headcount. One was the database that tracked all RSVPs and details about how folks were getting to D.C. The other, and much more complicated part, was the bus-tracking database, through which we tracked and coordinated the 2,200 buses that headed to D.C. for January 21.

   We scaled up this system in a few weeks. Our unbelievably dedicated volunteers, led by Director of Volunteers Caitlin Ryan, donated coding, field organizing, and database management skills to help this machine run! Operation Headcount was featured on *The Rachel Maddow Show* within a few hours of its launch and had so many people accessing it that it temporarily overwhelmed Google's platform.

JENNA   When we got about a week out, I think, we started putting out some content about the rules around how to go to protests and about nonviolence: If you're bringing signs, make sure that they're not on two-by-fours, make sure that they're on materials that are safe and can't be used as a weapon. And there were people who had been planning on going but now were definitively dropping out. There were definitely women who started dropping out because of security concerns.

The organizers come together in the final days before the march. From left: De'Ara Balenger, Meredith Shepherd, Vanessa Ruble, Carmen Perez, Tamika Mallory, Linda Sarsour, Ginny Suss, Tabitha St. Bernard-Jacobs, Jenna Arnold, and Daria Hall.

Washington, D.C.

BREANNE   And the clear backpacks! We announced that we would only allow clear backpacks, as a security measure. Within hours, clear backpacks were sold out everywhere, even on Amazon. I'm sure they were not expecting that. It was all so surreal. Our march created a bus shortage, a clear backpack shortage, and a pink yarn shortage!

BY CINDI LEIVE

OPTIMISM, INTERRUPTED

Albert Einstein famously said that the most important thing each of us must decide for ourselves is whether the universe is a friendly or an unfriendly place. I had always believed the former—that despite its horrors, the world tilts, slowly but inexorably, toward progress. I was an optimist. I thought the best of people. It informed everything I did.

The election took that certainty away from me.

The march brought it back—in newer, wiser form.

I was one of those much-mocked idealists crushed on the morning of November 9. After all, I'd blithely told a reporter just a week before that I thought that come mid-November, Donald Trump would be "getting smaller by the second in the rearview mirror." There was his open courtship of white supremacists and his flagrant misogyny, both denounced even by many in his party. There was his epic ineptness; surely no one who had watched him stumble through the debates could find him presidential. And there was, of course, the overweening cruelty that was his hallmark: mocking people with disabilities, taunting his opponents, ridiculing a Gold Star mom. I had hoped this would be damning: Wasn't the Golden Rule, or a version of it, the one common shared teaching among all religions? As my family headed to the Javits Center on November 8 for what we were sure would be Hillary Clinton's victory party, my eleven-year-old son asked me what would happen if Trump won. "He can't win," I said confidently. ("Well, Mom, he *can*," he pointed out.) Watching the results felt dislocating: like taking a step onto a well-trod stair that suddenly was not there. In the pre-dawn hours the next morning, messaging with a friend who had spent eighteen months working to mobilize the Latino vote, I said in disbelief, "I never believed all that 'two Americas' stuff. Even *now* it is hard to believe this is what half our population wants."

I know how sheltered it all sounds. In a *Saturday Night Live* episode that aired the following weekend, one skit featured a group of friends watching the election results. The women, all white, are shocked. "Oh my God," gasps the actress Cecily Strong, "I think America is racist."

Cindi Leive is the former editor–in–chief of *Glamour* and *Self*.

A white male partygoer is outraged: "This is the most shameful thing America has ever done!" he exclaims—at which point the black actors Dave Chappelle and Chris Rock collapse in uncontrollable hysterics. "C'mon, get some rest," Rock, rolling his eyes, tells the crowd. "You've got a big day of moping and writing on Facebook tomorrow."

I didn't spend the next day moping and writing on Facebook. I spent it grieving for an image of America I started to believe had only existed in my head, where my neighbors—both the ones I agreed with and the ones I didn't—were fundamentally good-hearted.

January 21 felt like a miracle. I boarded a D.C.-bound bus with fifty of my friends and colleagues, along with my fourteen-year-old daughter and her friends—it was my birthday, and there was no better party. The highways were crowded with buses crammed full of pink hats; the L'Enfant Plaza Metro station was so jammed that we spent a good hour underground, chanting and patiently inching our way toward the exit. The woman next to me held a sign that read, "My Husband's Chemo Costs $10,000 a Month"; she explained that she'd never been to a protest before, but that the health-care issue had compelled her to show up. "And also," she added, "the misogyny." The misogyny was what tied all our interests together, but what was magical about the march was that it made visible the fact that we *had* so many interests. There were grandmothers and grown men, church groups and unions, indigenous women and Black Lives Matter demonstrators.

Years before, at a reproductive-rights march, my husband and I had spotted a sign that read, "We came down on buses to save our uteruses." We'd found it hilarious, and he'd made me a T-shirt for that January day with the slogan on the front. But as I pressed through the crowd with my daughter, the shirt felt entirely insufficient—a glib remnant of another time. We, women, were not here for our uteruses. We were here for our *lives*, for other women's lives, for our souls and the soul of our country.

And there were so, so many of us. The universe felt friendly again. Or more properly: The universe felt bound together by people willing to work for a friendly planet—by speaking out over and over again, and not just on the issues we call our own. The year since the march has brought regular ugliness: Those were my fellow Americans lighting torches in Charlottesville and cheering the government's vicious anti-immigrant moves. But I know which vision of our country I choose to believe in, and if the millions of us who showed up on that January day, in big cities and small towns, keep showing up—to protest, to run for office, to vote—I think it can be made real.

I'm still an optimist. After all, Einstein wrote that if we *do* believe the universe is unfriendly, we'll spend our lives "creating bigger walls to keep out the unfriendliness and bigger weapons." We have an administration dedicated to doing just this. "But if we decide that the universe is a friendly place," he continued, "then we will use our technology, our scientific discoveries and our natural resources to create tools and models for understanding that universe. Because power and safety will come through understanding its workings and its motives."

The Women's March helped us understand. The world will continue to spin forward, but only if we push.

VIOLENT
ENDS

EVEN WE
KNOW
BETTER

Washington, D.C.

San Francisco

JAN 16–20, 2017

THE WATERGATE: PREPARING FOR MARCH DAY

IN THE DAYS BEFORE THE MARCH, THE ORGANIZERS WORKED FROM THE INFAMOUS WATERGATE HOTEL. THE NATIONAL TEAM TRAVELED TO WASHINGTON TO JOIN JANAYE INGRAM AND HER TEAM OF ORGANIZERS AND VOLUNTEERS, OVERSEEING LOGISTICS AND OPERATIONS IN THE DISTRICT OF COLUMBIA. AS THE ACTIVISTS DOVE INTO THEIR LAST DAYS OF PLANNING, THEY SHARED TENSE ELEVATOR RIDES WITH ENTHUSIASTIC TRUMP INAUGURATION ATTENDEES, DEALT WITH ONLINE HARASSMENT, AND FACED CRITIQUES WITHIN THEIR COALITION.

JENNA I remember showing up at the Watergate Hotel the week before the march. I mean, the irony of us being based at the Watergate Hotel while planning the largest human rights protest in history has to be mentioned.

NANTASHA To my knowledge the Women's March decided to stay at the Watergate because, simply put, they had the most available rooms to accommodate us and were willing to work with us on numerous things. The Women's March was a very last-minute, rushed thing, so we were scrambling and had been in talks with many hotels to work out the best deal given all the complexities. Trump supporters were all over D.C. that weekend, so it would have been really hard to avoid them altogether.

TAMIKA That was a very, very intense week. We had received death threats. Linda, specifically, was under attack. So much hate coming at us from so many different directions. Being in the hotel with Trump supporters wasn't easy.

JENNA We didn't want anyone knowing that we were at the Watergate. We didn't know what the reaction would be. So yeah, so it was definitely confidential. But it was really hard because it was swarming with people with red hats.

ALYSSA We got death threats on Twitter. They said they were happy for their Second Amendment rights because they were going to be able to use them on us and the people onstage.

CASSADY Hate crimes had increased following the election. The visibility of the march brought a new level of intensity to the online harassment and death threats. A certain element felt emboldened now. We were days away from a new administration that had promised to unleash hell on so many communities, so there was a menacing element, like: Soon we'll be able to get you.

LINDA In 2003, I was with my son, who was four years old at the time, in line at a bank in Brooklyn. It was winter, and I was wearing a long black coat and a black hijab. A middle-aged white man in the bank started yelling, "How can you serve people like this? They killed Americans. They are animals." He was looking directly at me, but I ignored him. He continued to scream and walk toward me, and my son was like, "Mommy, why is that man screaming at you? What did you do?" This is a four-year-old child. The man came directly next to me saying, "We will get rid of you all." One of the bank tellers asked him what he needed so she could get him the hell out. Eventually he left, but I felt so unsafe. My office was across the street, but I didn't go there. I jumped on a bus so he wouldn't follow us into the building.

Times are the same and maybe even worse than they were then. I don't want to see the threats. The vitriol is just draining. It's not that I'm

The partnership team meets in Carmen Perez's room in the Watergate Hotel.

Janaye Ingram, Director of Logistics, in the early hours before the march.

afraid of it, but it's draining. I wear hijab. And I'm from Brooklyn. There was a moment when I realized that I am this administration's worst nightmare. And not only that, but I also was resonating with people far and wide across this country.

MICHAEL One of my duties was security. I'll never do that again. It's an awful feeling knowing that there might be some car out there with a bomb. No insurance company would give us insurance. Thirteen companies denied us. I ended up calling my aunt, who's in the production side of the music business, to ask who insures Coachella, and I called that broker. The Friday before the rally, at five o'clock, he said, "You've got a deal—but this is the most expensive policy I've ever sold." This guy insures Coachella! It ended up being $108,000. For one day.

TAMIKA It was so intense. You know, just in terms of all of the stress. It was almost like we were in a bubble. There were moments when we were in that hotel, in the basement where it felt like being underwater at the bottom of the ocean.

MARIAM I kept running into Trump supporters and many Russians in the hotel and thought, Is this real?

NANTASHA It's so funny, thinking back, on the things that weren't negotiated until the last minute. Like, Oh, we need to have a little office space, right? We need to have some type of war room, or peace room, or something. And then negotiating with the hotel to give us that space for free.

TOSHI Janaye was doing all of these negotiations with the city through all of it. She is a badass, and in big meetings she would take out a map and say, "This is happening, and it's happening here."

JANAYE There was a whole range of emotions, staying at the Watergate. There was the very stark, contrasting reality of seeing people who were probably opposed to our very existence, who were also staying in the hotel and going to

---

MY MARCH

"WE WERE LITERALLY PHYSICALLY LIFTING UP THE WOMEN WHO CAME BEFORE US."

Attending the Women's March wasn't even a decision for me. The moment I saw on Facebook that some women were organizing a march, I immediately booked my ticket.

I've always considered myself an activist, and I think it's crucial for millennials to care about our government and the policies it shapes. I worked on Capitol Hill for Senator Claire McCaskill in 2009 because I wanted to advocate for legislation to fix our broken health care system. I lost my health care coverage in 2007, at age 21, when I got cancer and had to drop out of college to receive treatment. At the time, if you were over 18, you could only be insured under your parents if you were a full-time student.

I was raised by a family of feminist women. My father's mother was on the executive board of the League of Women Voters in St. Louis. The only thing I inherited from her was an antique sign that said "Women bring all the voters into the world. Let women vote." My mother's mother, Clara Jane Smith, was one of the first women to graduate from the University of Florida.

Gloria Steinem has this great quote where she says, "At my age, in this still-hierarchical time, people often ask me if I'm 'passing the torch.' I explain that I'm keeping my torch, thank you very much—and I'm using it to light the torches of others." It was my mother and grandmothers who lit *my* torch.

I went to the march with a group of seven women. The biggest thing for me was seeing all of the older women at the march who carried signs lamenting that they were still protesting for their rights. I was inspired by their dedication to continue to show up for so many years. At one point, in order to get closer to the speakers, we had to climb over a fairly large barricade—and there were some older women who couldn't jump over. So we younger women banded together, physically hoisting them up and over the wall together. We were literally lifting up the women who came before us. I felt such an immense amount of gratitude at that moment for those women.

POLLY RODRIGUEZ
30, New York City, entrepreneur and CEO,
marched in Washington, D.C.

Washington, D.C.

Los Angeles

balls. And we had the hotel staff saying to us, you know, "Please don't tell anyone you are here." They didn't want anyone to know that we were staying in the hotel, because they had all of these inaugural guests who were also there, and they felt it would hurt business.

MICHAEL   We were worried about security. We wanted to make sure that we were doing everything we possibly could to protect people. So we spent much of the week trying to get more security. But every firm in Washington was booked for the inauguration, and they didn't want their guys or their women to work 48 hours. So we ended up hiring officers out of Philadelphia. We bused them in, about 57 security officers—

mostly former police officers, civil service, FBI, and current officers off duty—so we had 175 in total, but that still wasn't enough.

MYSONNE LINEN, Head of Security The thing is, everyone needed to be safe. Not just those on the stage and the speakers, but the whole march. We had an entire plan for how security would be inserted into the crowd, how they would march in the crowd, the exit strategy for an emergency.

PAOLA One of the hardest moments for me was accepting the fact that my son Mateo wouldn't be able to go to the march. I knew the day of the march would be the busiest day for me. I also knew that Michael was going to be consumed filling in holes, so we had to make the decision to not bring our son on this historic day. I wish he could have seen in the flesh what his mama and papa did for him and his country. Mateo Ali wasn't able to be there with us on January 21, but it was his spirit, his joy, and his love that carried us through that historic day.

TONY Another thing I did was make sure people drank enough water. Movement people are terrible at taking care of themselves!

"WE MUST WORK HARDER TO MAKE PEOPLE AWARE THAT RACIAL BIAS AND GENDER BIAS CANNOT BE SEPARATED. THEY WORK TOGETHER."

ROWAN BLANCHARD, ACTIVIST AND ACTRESS

ONSTAGE IN LOS ANGELES

BREANNE It was insane. A few days before, the London lead called me to say, "Oh my God, they're telling us now that our march is too big. Our permit doesn't hold as many people as we're anticipating and now they're saying we can't march there." And this was, like, 48 hours before the march. And we decided, "Alrighty, let's go as high up as we can [laughs] and try to see how we can turn this around." We ended up getting approved through a petition in Parliament.

SARAH SOPHIE Three days before the march, someone told us we had to talk to this woman who knows all about Internet safety. She told us, "On the day of the march, your Internet is going to go down. What is your waterfall plan? Where is your auxiliary Internet? It has to be off-site, in a secured place. How are you dealing with emergencies?" We were terrified.

ALYSSA So we brought in the Digi Geeks, a superhero squad of kick-ass women of color working in social media and tech led by the extraordinary Stefanie Cruz. With less than 48 hours' notice, they came on as our trusty reinforcements to essentially run all social media while we were in the dark at the march.

MY MARCH

"IT COULD HAPPEN IN SWEDEN TOO."

In Stockholm we have something called the Stroller March that happens every year, to protest maternal mortality due to failures in reproductive health. This year they decided to combine the Stroller March with the Women's March. I went with two friends, one who is very politically active and the other who is from South Africa and had never been to a march. She was very open and curious. She asked us, "How do we as white women show support for women of color?" And my other friend said, "First, we just listen." The march was very calm and collected, as you would assume a Swedish political activity would be. There were a lot of signs about Trump and pussy hats, but there were also lots and lots of strollers.

The Women's March felt very different from the day after the election. In Sweden, that day was like a national day of mourning. My friends and colleagues all know I have U.S. and Finnish citizenship and that this election was personal for me. They were very supportive.

I had watched the election with friends from different countries. In Swedish we have an expression for staying up all night, *uppesittarkväll,* used for the night before Christmas Eve and election nights. We had planned one to celebrate when Hillary took the White House. We were all watching, and it got grimmer and grimmer. I took a taxi home at 4:30 in the morning, and it had snowed several feet. Sitting in the darkness and knowing Trump was taking the election—while zooming through the snow—was surreal, and terrible.

I was schooled in feminism at a women's college and read feminist work, but I never really identified with the word. Then when I was 24, I moved to Stockholm, where everybody is feminist. It's a widespread positive concept. *Of course, you're a feminist. What's the alternative?* So, soon after the election I joined a feminist group of Americans in Sweden. We wanted to talk with other Americans, so we didn't have to explain the context. One guy cried the whole time. But there was a good energy too. We agreed that what was happening in the U.S. was close to happening in France, and it could happen in Sweden too. We have a big neo-Nazi group in Sweden. So that has become our focus. We marched to say we won't let what's happening in the U.S. happen here.

JEN LINDBLAD
30, digital strategist, Stockholm;
marched in Stockholm

TAMIKA There were a lot of different issues coming up. I think during that week, we dealt with the antichoice issue.

TONY There were organizations that signed up through our website to be partners, and we were responding to them one by one. It wasn't working. I sent out a mass email, bcc'ing everyone and saying, "If you want to be a partner, please reply and confirm and we will add you to the list." Well, that may have been a mistake because some antichoice groups made it onto the list because their names were intentionally deceptive. The list should have been vetted better, but we were doing so much. From that point on, we did more extreme vetting of partners.

TAMIKA We also dealt that week with Clinton supporters wanting her name to be included in the list of historical women that we were uplifting. There was a lot happening all at once.

LINDA We chose not to invite Hillary or Bernie to speak. Nobody's "invited" to march. Bernie showed up on his own in Vermont. But De'Ara was in contact with Hillary—which is what people assumed wasn't happening. And not only were we in contact with her that morning, but she asked us, "How can I be helpful? Can I tweet in support of the Women's March?" We said, "Absolutely." So that day, she actually tweeted in support of us.

TAMIKA I've been in the movement for a long time. I've had the FBI knocking on my door at five in the morning. I've witnessed some very intense moments. Whether it be organizing the fiftieth anniversary of

"OUR CHILDREN WILL ASK US, 'WHERE WERE YOU WHEN OUR COUNTRY WAS THRUST INTO A LION'S DEN OF DEMAGOGUERY AND DIVISION?' AND WE WILL SAY, 'I STOOD WITH LOVE.'"

RABBI SHARON BROUS

ONSTAGE IN WASHINGTON, D.C.

the March on Washington, or the Million Man March twentieth anniversary. I've been in intense spaces where the work was constant and the stress level of everyone involved was up. But I have never, ever dealt with the intensity that we were in, in those last few days leading up to the march. And then the backdrop of that hotel, and what it represents in American history, was constantly looming.

I mean, I really found myself looking around my room for bugs. [*Laughs.*] I was looking behind the TV, in the light posts, looking for potential—you know, wiretapping. All of that was happening that week.

CARMEN The night before the march we gathered in a room and I asked everyone to hold hands. We said the Assata chant together and I felt a vibration of togetherness. We had all given our souls for this moment.

JENNA So at like six or seven the night before the march, I had a moment where I was like, You know what, we've done everything we can. All right, everyone, just put down your pencils, close your computers. That's it. We were literally turning it over to the universe. There was just this moment of calm. I had been prepared to work through the night. I said, "I need to get a proper meal and go to sleep." Which is not me—typically I'm hustling until the last minute. We all went up from the basement to go find food, and the lobby was packed with people dressed in black tie on the way to the inaugural ball. And that fucking sucked to see.

Setting up the stage in Washington, D.C., in the wee hours of January 21, 2017.

Three marchers
originally from Bahrain
in Washington, D.C.

BY ERIKA ANDIOLA

DON'T FORGET ABOUT US

Erika Andiola is on the staff of Our Revolution, an organization dedicated to revitalizing American democracy, empowering progressive leaders, and elevating the political consciousness.

The week leading up to the march was particularly tough for me because it was also the week before the inauguration. Those of us in the immigrant community knew that DACA [Deferred Action for Childhood Arrivals] could be rescinded the minute Trump took office (as indeed it was in the fall of 2017), and with me being a DREAMer and my entire family still undocumented, like so many other people, I knew it was going to be four years of hell. I was scared. My mom had been through deportation proceedings before.

I'd been an organizer in the immigrant community and then worked for Bernie Sanders' campaign. So when I was asked to speak at the Washington, D.C., march, I felt a lot of pressure, given that folks see me as a leader. What could I say, knowing that I didn't have all the answers but that people wanted hope? A lot of people have been negatively affected by the election, not just undocumented people. I had friends in the Muslim and transgender communities who were scared. What could I say to give all these people a sense of unity? Honestly, I am bad at writing speeches. So I said what was in my heart. I got up on the stage with my community and my family in mind. I told my own story, about my mom who decided to leave Mexico, the country where she was born and raised, to escape poverty and my father's abuse. She fled through the desert with her five children when I was 11. I shared how in 2013, as she was taken away by ICE [Immigration and Customs Enforcement] in handcuffs, she looked at me and said, "I'm gonna be fine." She was later released, and is now fighting to stay in the U.S. as a domestic abuse refugee.

My message, really, was don't forget about us. In the past I've faced a lot of frustration with the progressive movement. Many people didn't join us in the fight for DACA and against deportations when Obama was in office. So I saw making the speech in Washington as an opportunity to call on people to defend the rights of undocumented women and transgender women and others.

If I'd had a crystal ball the day of the march and I could have seen everything we've been able to accomplish despite all the opposition and attacks, I think I would have felt more hopeful. It's encouraging to me that the Women's March was not just a one-day thing but that it led people to organize on the local level, to run for local office, and to fight things like the Muslim ban. My hope today is that we don't burn out. That we can figure out a way to continue the momentum. It could be another three years. It's a marathon. For me, that marathon means working during the day to push the revolution *forward* with Sanders' ideas and then at night being on calls with Dreamers trying to push *back* against attacks on them. We have to seize the moment, and that requires a lot of work.

When I shared my mom's story at the march, she was in Arizona. She doesn't speak English, but she listened and heard "mom" in my speech; later she asked me what I'd said. My hope for the one-year anniversary of the march is that we will begin to hear new voices—not just the voices of DREAMers like me. I'd like to hear more stories of people like my mom.

MY MOM DOESN'T SPEAK ENGLISH, BUT SHE LISTENED AND HEARD "MOM" IN MY SPEECH; LATER SHE ASKED ME WHAT I'D SAID.

She is not a faceless stranger. She is Lupita Arreola, she is 59, and she has lived in Arizona for 20 years. She is a loving grandmother of seven children and a community leader who now fights for other immigrants like her who have to face the threat of detention and deportation every day. You don't see them on TV or speaking for themselves, but people like my mom and other immigrants have a lot to say. We have to keep telling their stories.

Washington, D.C.

Maryland AVE SW
300

THE FUTURE IS FEMALE

UNIFY + RISE

DISSENT IS PATRIOTIC

Washington, D.C.

THE
MARCH

Paris

JAN 20, 2017
11:00 P.M.

RISING UP, AROUND THE WORLD

AS INAUGURATION DAY CAME TO AN END, WOMEN'S MARCH ORGANIZERS PREPARED TO WELCOME A SPIRITED ASSORTMENT OF SEASONED ACTIVISTS, ARTISTS, CELEBRITIES, FORMER ARMCHAIR REVOLUTIONARIES, AND FIRST-TIME DEMONSTRATORS TO THE LARGEST SINGLE-DAY PROTEST IN HISTORY.

BOB   I was walking through the lobby of the Watergate, when Teresa Shook, the fire starter, the grandmother from Hawaii, came in. I think I was the first one to recognize her, and after nine tireless weeks of organizing together, it was such a magical moment to lock eyes for the first time. I could feel her love and appreciation from across the room, and getting to meet her in person made all of the trials of organizing worth it.

TED   I went over to a fast-food restaurant late at night before the march because I was starving. The general manager still happened to be there from the closing shift, so I knocked on the door and said, "Can I come in and buy a cup of coffee and some fries?"

And he let me. I said, "You know, you've got, like, a few hundred people out here who are working through the night to tear down the inaugural." He goes, "Yeah, I know. I wish we could sell 'em some food." And then I said, "And you've got a few hundred more coming in, to put up the Women's March." He was like, "Oh, I know. Normally we don't open up on a Saturday at five A.M. But tomorrow we're opening at five." They opened early for the march.

BREANNE   It's like the last leg of a marathon, where you're tired and exhausted, but then you're also nervous. All that week I had been meeting people for the first time who I had been talking to for months. And that was emotional. The moment that for me was the most emotional was when the march in Tokyo happened. Watching that one kick off, and seeing the little girls holding the signs in Japanese, and the families, and the communities marching together—it was just so moving. [More than 600 people, many of them expats, attended the march in Tokyo's Hibiya Park.] As soon as I saw Tokyo, I went down to the room where everyone was working, and I was just like, "You guys, the marches are starting. Tokyo's started." And everyone just stopped what they were doing and cheered, and it was so cool.

MYSONNE   I felt like a fly on the wall and I was so in admiration of everyone. Janaye had a "Do Not Disturb" sign posted beside her, Cassady was on the phone all the time, Michael was on his computer, everyone was focused on doing their part to create this moment in time.

LINDA   I had a feeling the march was going to be big, and I did not sleep the night before, because I had stayed up late to watch the live stream of New Zealand and Australia. 'Cause they're many hours ahead of us. And when I saw what was going down in Australia, I was like, whoa! If this is happening in Australia . . .

BREANNE   I was just watching it on Facebook Live and Twitter, and thinking, Oh my God, it's starting. It's happening. And then after Tokyo, it was Auckland, New Zealand, and then Australia. It hit me hard, like, wow. Tomorrow's going to be big.

A REAL WOMAN IS WHATEVER SHE WANTS TO BE

Sydney, Australia

Melbourne, Australia

Barcelona, Spain

JANAYE The night before the march, I didn't get any sleep really. I may have tried to take a one-hour nap, but my team had to be out at the site at midnight. That was the earliest that our setup could begin, and when we got to the site, they hadn't even started breaking down from the inauguration. I remember at a museum where we were, people were just leaving an inauguration ball and here we were, setting up for the march a few hours later. I had Ted Jackson doing ADA, Stacey Lee making sure the tents were up, Mike Dunn was handling transportation, Avery Jones was making sure everything arrived, Chris Cobbs was literally putting together bike racks. Melissa Mobley was a volunteer who came from Florida and was doing manual labor. It was an amazing collaboration.

Nairobi, Kenya

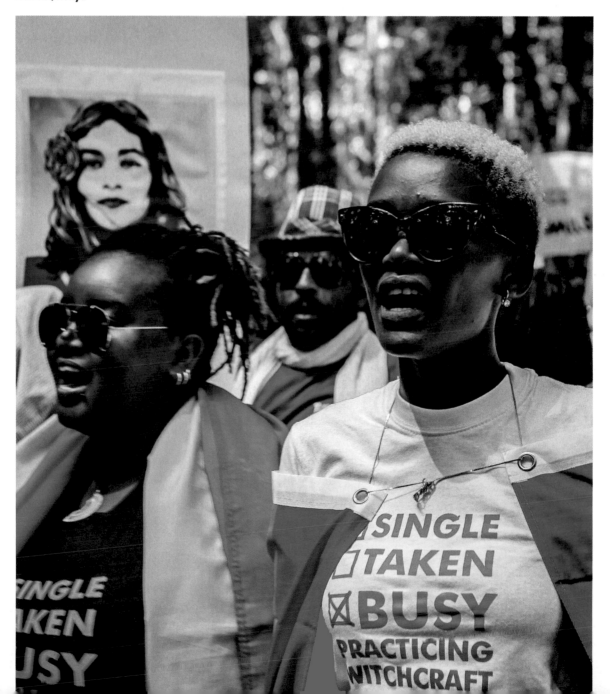

WE STAND

WITH OUR
AMERICAN
SISTERS

London

Berlin

Trafalgar Square in London

Ashley Judd onstage in
Washington, D.C.

THE ROAR

BY ASHLEY JUDD

Ashley Judd is an actress and political activist. She has a master's degree in political administration from Harvard's Kennedy School of Government.

I chose to sleep on the floor the night before I spoke at the march. I am a backcountry backpacker, and I needed to simulate being in my church, the cathedral of the woods. I was staying at a rented house in Washington with some of my closest girlfriends and two of their friends whom I'd never met. A sense of something sacred was building. Right before we left for the march, I asked to be alone. In a bedroom with hardwood floors, where I thought the acoustics would help me practice the projection I would need at the march, I boomed out the poem I was planning to read, "I Am a Nasty Woman" by Nina Donovan. It electrified the entire house for all of us. We were crying and we hadn't even left yet. That was the first whisper of the roar.

Backstage at the march, I bumped into Callie Khouri, my director from *Divine Secrets of the Ya-Ya Sisterhood*, while we were standing in line for the porta-potty. I recited some of the poem for her, and she began to weep. At one point I hopped onstage to look out over the vast crowd, to prepare myself visually for that gorgeous sea of pink I'd be addressing, and I pulled a technician aside and asked if I could do the poem for him. He cried. He said, "Thank you."

I knew it was going to be a transcendent moment. I had known the poem would be unifying and collectivizing from the moment a month before when I first heard Nina, a 19-year-old from Tennessee, recite it at a performance by youth poet laureates. It was seared into my brain that night. Nina slayed me. I bawled my way through her time onstage—"I am not as nasty as racism, fraud, conflict of interest, homophobia, sexual assault, transphobia, white supremacy, misogyny . . ."—and instantly knew I was going to do it at the march. I hadn't even been invited to speak yet! But I knew "Nasty Woman" belonged to everyone.

At the first words of the poem—"I am a *nasty woman!*"—the roar was a collective gasp. And then it went totally quiet and I knew people were listening so intently, and the more I let loose Nina's poem, the quieter it got. You could have heard a pin drop. In that silence I could feel the parts of the poem that resonated in very specific ways: "I am not as nasty as a swastika painted on a pride flag." And then later: "Electro Conversion Therapy, the new gas chambers shaming the gay out of America, turning rainbows into suicide notes." I heard grief in that silence.

And then it really started, a 360-degree rumble from way, way back in the crowd. I knew I had only a few minutes to speak, but I had to pause now and then because of the roar. And at the point in the poem that talks about bloodstains and tampons and pads being taxed while Rogaine and Viagra are not, the crowd went nuts. They couldn't believe that finally, in this huge public space, on all the television channels from C-SPAN to Fox, we could talk about *menstruation*. Of course, I was wearing white because that is the color of the suffrage movement. And I did that thing we do when we turn around to see if we've seeped through our clothes. It was amazing. The roar was a rumble, a wave, a crescendo, an aria. There was a visual to it as well. I could see the crowd react physically just as I could feel myself throwing my body into

THE ROAR WAS A RUMBLE, A WAVE, A CRESCENDO, AN ARIA. THERE WAS A VISUAL TO IT AS WELL. I COULD SEE THE CROWD REACT PHYSICALLY.

the performance. That roar was personal, political, spiritual, special.

I've taken a beating for this rendering of Nina's poem in some spaces, including being called mentally ill on Twitter and other forms of retaliation and retribution. But it's worth it. Far more of us, I know from experience, believe in equality, social justice, collaboration, and peace.

From the moment I first heard Nina's poem that night in Tennessee, I started to cry. The shattering grief I'd experienced after the election came flooding back up. Listening to this powerful young woman was both devastating and cathartic: She was so lucidly naming what was going on, and her youth gave me such fierce hope. The roar was my signal that the poem had felt that way for others too. A very young woman came up to me at the airline counter after the march and said, "'Nasty Woman' changed my life." It changed mine too. I cherish my memory of the roar. It's the proudest I've ever been.

"NASTY WOMAN"
BY NINA MARIAH DONOVAN

I am a nasty woman.

I'm not as nasty as a man who looks like he bathes in Cheeto dust. A man whose words are a diss track to America. Electoral college-sanctioned, hate speech contaminating this national anthem.

I'm not as nasty as Confederate flags being tattooed across my city. Maybe the South actually is going to rise again. Maybe for some it never really fell.

Blacks are still in shackles and graves, just for being black. Slavery has been reinterpreted as the prison system in front of people who see melanin as animal skin.

I am not as nasty as a swastika painted on a pride flag, and I didn't know devils could be resurrected but I feel Hitler in these streets. A mustache traded for a toupee. Nazis renamed the Cabinet. Electro Conversion Therapy, the new gas chambers shaming the gay out of America, turning rainbows into suicide notes.

I am not as nasty as racism, fraud, conflict of interest, homophobia, sexual assault, transphobia, white supremacy, misogyny, ignorance, white privilege. I'm not as nasty as using little girls like Pokémon before their bodies have even developed, I am not as nasty as your own daughter being your favorite sex symbol, like your wet dreams infused with your own genes.

But yeah, I'm a nasty woman—a loud, vulgar, proud woman.

I am not nasty like the combo of Trump and Pence being served up to me in my voting booth. I'm nasty like the battles my grandmothers fought to get me into that voting booth.

I'm nasty like the fight for wage equality. Scarlett Johansson, why were the female actors paid less than half of what the male actors earned last year? See, even when we do go into higher paying jobs our wages are still cut with blades sharpened by testosterone. Why is the work of a black woman and a hispanic woman worth only 63 and 54 cents of a white man's privileged daughter? This is not a feminist myth. This is inequality.

So we are not here to be debunked. We are here to be respected. We are here to be nasty.

I am nasty like my bloodstains on my bedsheets. We don't actually choose if and when to have our periods. Believe me, if we could some of us would. We don't like throwing away our favorite pairs of underpants. Tell me, why are tampons and pads still taxed when Viagra and Rogaine are not? Is your erection really more [important] than protecting the sacred messy part of my womanhood? Is the bloodstain on my jeans [not] more embarrassing than the thinning of your hair?

I know it is hard to look at your own entitlement and privilege. You may be afraid of the truth. I am unafraid to be honest. It may sound petty bringing up a few extra cents. It adds up to the pile of change I have yet to see in my country.

I can't see. My eyes are too busy praying to my feet hoping you don't mistake eye contact for wanting physical contact. Half my life I have been zipping up my smile hoping you don't think I want to unzip your jeans.

I am unafraid to be nasty because I am nasty like Susan, Elizabeth, Eleanor, Amelia, Rosa, Gloria, Condoleezza, Sonia, Malala, Michelle, Hillary!

And our pussies ain't for grabbing. They're for reminding you that our walls are stronger than America's ever will be.

Nina Mariah Donovan is a spoken-word artist and a student at Middle Tennessee State University.

Our pussies are for our pleasure. They are for birthing new generations of filthy, vulgar, nasty, proud, Christian, Muslim, Buddhist, Sikh, you name it, for new generations of nasty women. So if you a nasty woman, or you love one who is, let me hear you say, hell yeah.

WOMEN'S
MARCH
-ON WASHINGTON-

America Ferrera speaks in
Washington, D.C.

BY AMERICA
FERRERA

MARCHING FORWARD

The moment I stepped onto the stage in Washington, the energy from the crowd was overwhelming, unlike anything I have experienced. I've never spoken in front of 1.2 million people before, and I hadn't known what to expect.

I couldn't see the end of the crowd. I had no idea how many people I was talking to. It felt real and raw. Normally, I would have been nervous, but the purpose of being there was so clear that it carried me through. The thing that shook me was how much joy there was. It was a heartening of spirit that I think made everyone feel less alone and more human and more alive.

I needed this feeling, myself. I needed to know that there were so many of us who were ready to show up for this moment in history. It pulled me out of my lingering feelings of despair from the election. I still felt sad and daunted and shocked, but I also felt like there was a way forward.

At the root of it all was a sense of community. Everyone was high on an intoxicating combination of urgency and love. Community is something we lack in our culture these days. It's rare that we show up and stand with people, get in the same room together. So much is done digitally and quickly. I can't overemphasize how transformative it was to be in that crowd with so many other people who shared the same sense of passion and purpose.

It became very important to me to continue building community after the march. Our culture works against being able to sit in a room with people whose experiences are different from our own but whose hopes and dreams for the future are shared. This is what the Women's March was about. Since the march I have tried to grow my circle of community far and wide. We have shared some victories and bolstered each other through setbacks.

To move forward as a movement, we have to stay connected to the reason we marched in the first place: one another. It doesn't make sense

America Ferrera is an Emmy-winning actress who is currently a producer and star of *Superstore*.

to march and donate and then go back to our lives, shut off from what's uncomfortable or unfamiliar to us. We need to challenge ourselves to show up in community with an open heart.

After the march, my husband and I started gathering our friends, many of whom are artists and storytellers, together with friends who are activists on the front lines in order to bridge those communities. Our gatherings grew into an organization called Harness. We bring people together in the hope that those wanting to use their voices can do it from a deeper, more rooted place, because they are invested in real, personal relationships. That's the fuel. The people you meet, the bodies you hug, the stories you hear. We don't have to worry about people going home and forgetting what they heard and what they need to do. You don't forget about people you know and love—you carry them in your heart. That's what's at the core of the magical experience I had at the Women's March. If we can bring that ethic of community and love into our daily lives, I believe we can sustain a movement beyond a single historical day.

PUSSY
grabs
back

PUSSY
grabs
back

London

Washington, D.C.

JAN 21, 2017 3:00 A.M.

MARCH DAY: BREAKING RECORDS, MAKING HISTORY

A FEW HOURS BEFORE DAWN, JUST 74 DAYS AFTER A GROUP OF CONCERNED WOMEN CAME TOGETHER TO FORM THE WOMEN'S MARCH TEAM, THE ORGANIZERS REALIZED THAT THE NUMBERS IN WASHINGTON WOULD BE MORE MASSIVE THAN THEY HAD ANTICIPATED. LATER THAT DAY THEY WATCHED AS THE CROWD, WHICH THEY HAD INITIALLY THOUGHT MIGHT BE 200,000, BALLOONED TO AN ESTIMATED 800,000 TO 1.2 MILLION PEOPLE.

EMMA   Mrinalini and I had cried, laughed, and become sisters without ever having met in person until we got to D.C. In our mission to park a record number of buses, we had discovered secret parking lots, we had bartered agreements with private homeowners for lots, we had begged, cajoled, and pleaded with bus companies and permitting agencies. We had made hand-drawn bus signs. We joked that our mission was to "leave no granny behind."

As the buses began arriving in D.C., our plan was put to the test. I remember at five o'clock on the morning of the march, Mrinalini actually had to physically track down and wake up a sleeping parking-lot owner to unlock the gates for buses to park.

GINNY   The day of the march, we were on-site from maybe 3 A.M., and I think I looked up for the first time around 6 A.M. and I saw all of these women. And not only did I see people with the Amplifier art, but I saw the pink pussy hats everywhere. And I, along with some of the other fellow organizers, had been super negative about the pussy hats [see story on page 257.]. I was instantly put off by the fact that the hat was pink. Not only do I not love associating pink as a girly, feminine color—because I think it restricts and pigeonholes what it means to be feminine—I also think that not everyone's pussy is pink. I know a whole lot of people who don't have pink pussies.

But I will say that I have to give them credit. Because when I looked up at 6 A.M., four hours before we were going to start the rally, and saw people with signs that they had made themselves, and they had Amplifier art, and they had those hats, and you looked out at this sea of pink hats everywhere, it really was an incredible way to unify a super-diverse and disparate crowd of women and men marching. That it was a woman offering up a pattern, and that all of these people had made them by hand all across the country—that was very cool. I didn't realize it until afterward.

EMMA There were people as far as you could see all the way up to the Capitol. There were so many components that were unexpected, like the pink hats. We knew the pink hats were a thing, but we didn't realize they would be what they were. No idea. It was just kind of one of those things, like the way we were expecting something like 300,000 people in D.C. and it was nearly a million that came out.

SARAH SOPHIE By 8:30 A.M. there were so many people that we had lost Internet

"WHEN IT GETS HARDER TO LOVE, LET'S LOVE HARDER."

VAN JONES, AUTHOR AND COFOUNDER OF THE DREAM CORPS

ONSTAGE IN WASHINGTON, D.C.

Organizers onstage in
Washington, D.C.

Organizers Jasmine Blackmon,
Tabitha St. Bernard-Jacobs,
and Cassady Fendlay march.

Washington, D.C.

completely. But an anonymous member of Congress had given the Digi Geeks access to the Longworth House Office Building. And they walked over there and basically controlled the whole operation from a conference table. At one point, the Porta-Potties couldn't get services. Would you believe the Porta-Potties were called *Don's Johns*? We had to share them with the inauguration.

I was in charge of our outfits, and if you notice, we're all wearing black with the jackets Patagonia generously donated to us. One of the many things I was in charge of was our look. [*Laughs.*] And not even in a silly way, but just because we knew these were going to be historical images and we wanted to look somewhat uniform.

We didn't want to look at those photos 20 years from now and think, Gosh, I wish I hadn't worn that. We wanted something simple that photographed well that we weren't going to be embarrassed about.

PAOLA   By 8:30 A.M., we could not get on social media. So we didn't have any clue about what was going on across the rest of the country and across the world. All we knew was the sea of pink hats we saw in front of us. And we were astounded and crazed by the numbers.

CARMEN   It was my fortieth birthday and I'd been working so hard the whole week that I'd forgotten. My birthday is always a hard day for me because my older sister was buried on my seventeenth birthday. But my two favorite couples—my mom and dad and Mr. B and his wife, Pam—called me that day and I got so emotional. Then someone announced my birthday to the crowd and everyone sang to me—I was so embarrassed!

JANAYE   I spoke with the commanding officer from Metropolitan Police Department in Washington, D.C., and I told him that as of the night before, Sam and Operation Headcount had projected our numbers would be over 800,000. The officer chuckled and said he had been monitoring numbers and thought we would have somewhere around 300,000 to 350,000 people. As the day went on, I remember walking on the stage and looking out at streets were overwhelmed with people. One of our security team pulled me aside and said, "If you think that's amazing, turn around."

When I turned around, the whole street behind the stage was a wall of people, and people were pouring over the hill. When I saw Leonard Lee of the National Park Service, whom I have worked with many times. He smiled and asked me where and how we planned to march. I laid out for him that we were going to use our marshals to direct people to the side streets and have everyone march from Constitution Avenue to Pennsylvania Avenue. An hour or so passed before a member of the mayor of Washington, D.C.'s staff said there were concerns about us marching. She asked me to speak to the mayor, and we learned that since our last conversation, people had overwhelmed all of the side streets that we were planning to use. We were unsure if our marshals would be able to lead people to the Ellipse without microphones or other sound equipment. Everyone was concerned that people might be crushed, and we debated whether it was safe to march.

TAMIKA That morning I stood on the stage and I looked out at the crowd. And I was so overcome by emotion. My reaction was, Oh, shit. Look what we did. This is amazing. And then that feeling turned into sadness.

I was standing next to Sybrina Fulton, Trayvon Martin's mother. And I looked, and I . . . I just realized for a minute that if I had died—the way Trayvon was killed, the way Sandra Bland was arrested for nothing and died in a prison cell—if Tamika Mallory was any of those people [killed by racialized state or vigilante violence], the women and the families who showed up in D.C. on march day would never, ever have come together in that way for me. They wouldn't have been there for me any more than they were there for Trayvon or Sandra.

And so I went from a feeling of, like, this is beautiful, to a sad place of, Wow: this is the power we have. Yet it is not being exercised on behalf of the rights of all. And particularly not on behalf of black and brown folks. And I was a little bitter for a minute, you know? I think I carried that with me for a while, even after the march.

GINNY Janelle Monáe's management at her record company, Wondaland, recommended that she perform the song "Hell You Talmbout," which is her song dedicated to victims of police violence. She called out by name many of the victims who have been killed from police violence. She brought some of her other Wondaland artists, I believe Jidenna was at the Women's March singing with her onstage, St. Beauty were there, and they're incredible. It was very much in the tradition of call-and-response. She called out the names, encouraged the audience to say them with her, and it was just a really beautiful tribute to victims of police violence.

TOSHI I'm the music director, but I was moving all over the place. It was very

---

MY MARCH

"I FELT LIKE I WAS IN THE CROWD, LIKE I WAS MARCHING."

I learned about the march on social media. I knew of the grievances about Trump's insensitivity toward women, immigrants, and minority groups—and his sexist language and degrading behavior. I took part in the march virtually, in a hotel room in Addis Ababa. The regime won't let us assemble. But you can't arrest me on my Facebook wall.

I was marching in solidarity with the sisters in the USA, but I was also marching for the women like me who live under oppressive governments and can't march. I had studied Hillary Clinton and the influence of the U.S. in advancing democratic practices and championing women. To see this end in the USA with Trump's election affects our well-being and our society in Ethiopia.

The young feminist movement in Africa is very strong. We have been able to create alternative spaces, enabled by social media. For over seven years now, we have been sharing our daily experiences on Facebook. The opposition saw this as young idle women talking randomly. But these "young idle women" have now gained the attention of the leaders. Our successes may seem slow, but if we are now able to talk about taboo subjects like abortion, someday we can get women access to reproductive health care and rights.

On the Saturday of the Women's March, I dedicated that day to the march and announced on my Facebook that I would be marching. I watched live on CNN. I wish I could have marched physically, but connecting virtually blurred away the distance. I was busy tweeting my mind out. Listening to CNN, watching, tweeting in verses. *I march for myself, my safety, and to be a voice for change. I march for the millions of women and girls who live under the worst form of dictatorship and tyranny. I march because my government is legalizing and normalizing state-sponsored violence and policing of women's bodies. I march because it is my human and democratic right to march against injustice.*

I felt like I was in the crowd, like I was marching. It's hard to fully describe. It was incredibly emotional. I was online for four hours. CNN was showing people in different states. One million. Then two. Then three. Wow. In D.C. alone 1 million. Those millions meant a lot. We were telling the leaders of the world that enough is enough.

ZONEZIWOH MBONDGULO-WONDIEH
32, executive director of Women for a Change Cameroon; "marched" in Addis Ababa, Ethiopia

Washington, D.C.

The Washington Monument
seen from the Mall.

"I WANT TO TELL THE CHILDREN NOT TO BE AFRAID, BECAUSE WE ARE NOT ALONE. THERE ARE STILL MANY PEOPLE THAT HAVE THEIR HEARTS FILLED WITH LOVE."

**SOPHIE CRUZ,
ACTIVIST, AGE 6**

ONSTAGE IN WASHINGTON, D.C.

Washington, D.C.

A march attendee wears
a dress made out of fabric
printed with Amplifier art,
Washington, D.C.

The Capitol South Metro Station in Washington, D.C.

Singer Alicia Keys performs in Washington, D.C.

**Janelle Monáe performs with
St. Beauty in Washington, D.C.**

difficult to control the desperateness of some people to stay onstage. Fifty people would be on the stage, and to get them off and keep the performance on track timewise . . . it was unbelievable.

Taina Asili's song "War Cry" is when the whole thing came together, when the sound got really good. Everyone did a great job from a musical standpoint, but when her song hit, the energy of the stage elevated and everyone started firing on all cylinders and everything started to move—boom, boom, boom—really well. Most of the songs weren't rehearsed, and everybody kicked it at the march. And Taina got up there, no rehearsal. It was one of my favorite moments.

LINDA Charlie Brotman was the announcer for every inauguration for the past 60 years before Trump's people fired him. He was devastated about his dismissal, and as if that wasn't enough, his wife had died recently. I told the Women's March family that I was going to find him so he could announce the march, and I did. The joy he exuded was remarkable. He brought out the best in all of us. He was happy from the deepest of his

AS A
WOMAN
IS
UNFREE

"-AUDRE LORDE

Chattanooga, Tennessee

"MY LIBERATION IS LINKED TO THE UNDOCUMENTED TRANS LATINA . . . THE DISABLED STUDENT . . . THE SEX WORKER."

**JANET MOCK,
WRITER, TV HOST AND
TRANSGENDER RIGHTS ADVOCATE**

WASHINGTON, D.C.

core and that made me happy. He said he would never forget that day, and we will never forget him.

JANAYE By noon there were people everywhere. It wasn't possible to get anyone through the crowds, much less identify an end point for the crowd. At the suggestion of the officers who had communication with other officers in the crowd, we changed our position and made a decision that we would no longer march. Vanessa and I started talking through how we would communicate our decision to the people who had come such a long way to march. I went back onstage to inform other members of our team. I could hear people chanting, "*Let us march!*"

In that moment, I knew I *had* to devise a way for us to be able to march. In the weeks of planning, I heard so many stories of women who were coming with their mothers and daughters, women in wheelchairs, women who marched with Dr. King, who were coming together in this moment to march. It was so important for these women to be able to have the full experience that I knew if we didn't figure out how to make a way for them to march, we would potentially be putting more people in harm's way.

At 2 P.M. I went back to Leonard Lee and said, "We have to figure out a way to have people march." He asked me again what the plan would be. I told him I would make an announcement from the stage and we would go back to the plan of having people walk toward Pennsylvania Avenue and then down to the Ellipse. He said he would ready the National Park officers and we let Metropolitan Police know. Next, I communicated with the mayor's office to make sure she knew that we were going to march. I asked our marshals to be prepared and I made the announcement from the stage. When we finished our programming and the march began, it was peaceful and safe and people who wanted to march and came from all over the country were able to.

TOSHI I tell people the stage was like a belly button and it was holding everything together, and then the whole thing stood up and started to walk away.

JENNA I sort of knew in my bones—and it was a feeling that carried me through the whole eight weeks of preparation—that this was going to be bigger than people were expecting. I also knew in my bones that it

Janet Mock takes a selfie with (from left) organizers Nantasha Williams and Brea Baker.

Washington, D.C.

Washington, D.C.

Organizers onstage in Washington, D.C.

Sophie Cruz with her parents, Raul and Zoyla, and her younger sister at the Women's March.

was going to be OK. And D.C. happened exactly as I thought it would. I knew there would be an overwhelming number of people. I knew we were going to barely get it together. I knew we would just get across the finish line, and with plenty of things having fallen through the cracks.

I had gotten up at two the morning of the march like a pregnant woman in her first trimester who can't sleep. Waves of relief, grief, anger, fear came throughout the day. Finally we started marching, and I was with my brother and my best friend, but I ended up losing them

both in the crowd. I ended up sort of walking—as we all did, which is this beautiful image—we were all on the line together at the march.

MICHAEL Trump had masterfully built this Make America Great Again brand, stirring up racial and gender anxiety in this country and making white men in particular feel like they'd been left behind. On that amazing Saturday, the Women's March succeeded in telling a different story about America, about how women are leaders and women are resilient. The march showed us that women are persistent, and that women will show up and rise above an election where we saw and heard the most nasty, misogynistic, sexist, vicious views and attacks on women that we've ever seen in a presidential election.

PAOLA Only later did we—Sarah Sophie, Linda, Carmen, Tamika, Alyssa, and a bunch of the other organizers—all march together to the Washington Monument. Then I went to the White House, to the Ellipse, and saw all the signs that were posted: "This is what democracy looks like." "I am not free while any woman is unfree." "We are the granddaughters of the witches you could not burn." People were dancing. It was a living museum.

The ironic thing was that a group of us had spent weeks trying to come up with a final action for people, a kind of exclamation point at the end of the march. We were going to have people put down red roses. Or books. Or we were going to have a cool choir. But we couldn't decide on anything. And so when I walked up to the Ellipse and I saw what had happened naturally—all the homemade signs, the gathering—it was exactly the thing that we didn't know how to create, but the people had created it.

"I DIDN'T COME HERE TO BE IN A PARADE. WE CAN PARADE WHEN WE WIN . . . UNTIL THEN LET'S RESIST AND SAY BLACK LIVES MATTER!"

MALKIA CYRIL, FOUNDER AND EXECUTIVE DIRECTOR, CENTER FOR MEDIA JUSTICE

ONSTAGE IN SAN FRANCISCO

SARAH SOPHIE Something about my nine-year-old daughter standing with me humbled me and brought me right into the moment. And that was the only time I cried that day. She was with me all day, right at my side, instructing Alyssa and me on all the notable YouTubers and TV people who we didn't recognize. She was there by my side helping emergency

MY SISTER CAN DO ANYTHING I CAN DO

WE ARE THE LEADERS WE'VE BEEN LOOKING FOR.
JOIN US • LOVEARMY.ORG

WE ARE THE LEADERS WE'VE BEEN LOOKING FOR.
JOIN US • LOVEARMY.ORG

#LOVE ARMY

Washington, D.C.

Gwen Carr, mother of Eric Garner, who died after being placed in a chokehold by New York City police.

vehicles through to a woman in labor, helping route the crowd via Twitter to the correct march route. She was next to me onstage singing "Ella's Song." She was sharing her chocolate bar sitting next to Gloria Steinem and Sybrina Fulton. She held the banner and marched with us. She chanted with us, and her small head just barely grazed the top of the Women's March banner. I had been nervous about my kids coming to the march, and in fact, my other two children stayed behind; one was sick and the other was too young to handle the crowds. I never said it out loud—I whispered it to my husband over the phone days before the march—but I was worried. But in the moment, marching with my daughter, nothing has ever felt more right.

BREANNE In just one month, we had gone from 20 cities to 200, with marches happening on every continent. I won't ever forget when we confirmed Antarctica. It was a feeling that encompassed your core, knowing that this was just so much bigger than we had ever dreamed. This wasn't just about one person or one administration; this was about access to education in Asia, gender violence in South America, equal representation in Australia, reproductive health in Europe, clean water in Africa, climate change in Antarctica . . . this was about women standing up for their rights from every corner of the world.

MY MARCH

"I WANTED MY DAUGHTER TO SEE THAT HER MOTHER DIDN'T JUST STAND BY."

I live in central Illinois in a fairly conservative county. I never thought of myself as an activist before, but I work as a web developer, so when I see a problem, I think about how to solve it. If I feel I can help make it better, then I will become involved.

A friend of mine heard about local activists who had organized an overnight bus to D.C. I have a young daughter—she's nine. I knew from the moment I boarded that bus that I was marching not just for me, but for her. The fact that she will grow up and become a young woman during the Trump years is not lost on me. I wanted her to see that her mother didn't just stand by when women's rights were being threatened—that she actually did something about it. I wanted her to see exactly how to use your voice and your vote to protect our rights.

I won't ever forget the feeling when the bus arrived in a parking lot about six blocks from the Capitol. There were more than two dozen buses parked there. One bus after another, after another, arriving. I was in awe of how organized the whole thing was. I felt the great power women hold in this country.

As we marched down Pennsylvania Avenue, in a huge throng of people, chanting "We will not go away—welcome to your first day!" I felt the power of the voices, echoing off the buildings, speaking directly to our lawmakers. It was the most empowered I have ever felt as a citizen.

The image of one man will never leave me. He was in a wheelchair, holding a sign that said "Mock me to my face." He had the most confident, powerful expression on his face. As everyone marched past him, they cheered—and I felt a sense of relief that even in this, a time that felt so dark, humanity would show up.

MELANIE J.
46, Bloomington, Illinois, web developer;
marched in Washington, D.C.

GLORIA Of course, I knew the march was contagious, but definitely not that it would stretch coast-to-coast, from big cities to small towns, and become the biggest march in this nation's history. Or that it would spread to other countries on every continent. This only began to dawn on me as I got emails during the march from, say, a small town in Oklahoma, or a big city in Germany, Kenya, or India. I was especially moved by people gathering at the Brandenburg Gate in Berlin, where the Berlin Wall had so tragically divided Germany. They knew about Trump's threat to build a wall against Mexico, and they said, "Tell Americans that walls don't work!" I did convey their message when I spoke at the march.

MRINALINI I think the one thing that the Women's March definitely proved was that this was not a coastal movement. There were marches that happened in the

Marching in Washington, D.C. (from left): YoNasDa Lonewolf, Arrow Marie Peretz (daughter of march organizer Sarah Sophie Flicker), Flicker, organizer Alyssa Klein.

Washington, D.C.

"We are collective agents of history," civic rights activist Angela Davis told the crowd in Washington, D.C.

heartland. Like Oklahoma City has never seen a march that is 15,000 people strong, right? That is unheard of. Kansas saw marches of like 8,000, 9,000 people. South Carolina. Some of the biggest marches were actually not on the coast. Chicago was the third largest, with over a quarter of a million people. Saint Paul, Minnesota, was over 100,000. So we broke records in all of the different cities that we were in.

PAOLA No one would have imagined that by January 21, one day after the inauguration, we would be celebrating, we would be dancing, we would feel triumphant, and we would feel like we won. We got knocked down as a nation, as a country, as a people, as individuals. But it's not about getting knocked down. It's about how you rise up.

I MARCH FOR MY DAUGHTER

St. Paul, Minnesota

DIVERSITY IS THE WAY

T MARCH

Women's Rights
RIGHTS

GIRL

Anchorage, Alaska

Boise, Idaho

Gloria Steinem,
Washington, D.C.

Chicago

Washington, D.C.

"THE PRESIDENT IS NOT AMERICA. HIS CABINET IS NOT AMERICA . . . WE ARE AMERICA. AND WE ARE HERE TO STAY."

**AMERICA FERRERA,
ACTRESS AND CHAIR,
WOMEN'S MARCH ARTISTS' TABLE**

ONSTAGE IN WASHINGTON, D.C.

BY JESSICA
GONZÁLEZ-ROJAS

SALUD.
DIGNIDAD.
JUSTICIA.

As I stood at the edge of the stage that January day in Washington, I scanned the enormous and beautiful crowd and caught sight of our *poderosas* (activists) piled atop a van just to the left of the stage. My heart leaped with joy and relief, knowing that the bus of poderosas from Miami, many of whom were undocumented, had arrived safely. They screamed and cheered as I spoke, ferociously waving signs that read "Salud. Dignidad. Justicia."

I'm the leader of the National Latina Institute for Reproductive Health (NLIRH), and I had decided to support the Women's March once three fierce women of color were named in its leadership. As the march was first being organized, I worked alongside several other reproductive justice leaders to connect the cochairs with the reproductive health, rights, and justice movement and garner support for the march on a national level.

What is reproductive justice? For NLIRH and our Latinx poderosas, it will be attained when all people—including women of color, low-income people, LGBTQ people, young parents, and immigrants—have the economic, social, and political power and means to make decisions about their body, sexuality, health, and family. (*Latinx* is the gender-neutral term we use to challenge the Spanish language's gender binary.)

It's crucial to understand that a person's intersecting identities determine access to power and resources, and that systems deny access based on identity. Reproductive justice seeks to identify, name, and dismantle these systems of oppression. Reproductive justice means that I, as a Latina, a mother, and a queer person; as a daughter of an immigrant father and a Puerto Rican mother; and as a leader, can stand with all my identities and fight for freedom. I marched with passion to protect all people's fundamental human right to *salud, dignidad y justicia*—health, dignity, and justice.

I marched in the Women's March for Blanca Borrego, an undocumented Latina mother of three from Houston, who sat two

Jessica González-Rojas is the executive director of the National Latina Institute for Reproductive Health.

hours in the waiting room of her gynecologist's office for a follow-up appointment, only to be brought back to the exam room and met by Harris County Sheriff's deputies. Instead of receiving the critical reproductive health care she needed from a caring physician, Blanca was arrested in front of her daughters, one of whom said that the sheriff's deputies announced that they planned to deport her. She was robbed of her dignity and her human right to health care. Viewing this horrific event through a reproductive justice framework, we see the multiple, intersecting systems of oppression that conspired to facilitate her arrest.

But Blanca's story is just one of countless stories of denial of justice and basic human rights for immigrant women and families in this country. I also marched for a thirty-two-year-old Latina and mother of three from Texas whose name I cannot share. She was forced to borrow money from friends, pawn possessions, and take out a payday loan with exorbitant interest rates to cover the cost of her abortion. As she struggled to raise the funds, the price of her procedure rose higher with each passing week. When she finally had the resources ready, she had to take an unpaid week off work to travel three and a half hours to a clinic. There she had to adhere to Texas law, which requires multiple unnecessary appointments to create a mandatory delay before an abortion. The hurdles she faced were unjust and inhumane.

As the poet activist Audre Lorde stated, we do not live single-issue lives. As the march came together, we witnessed the development of a platform that was intersectional. Activists for reproductive justice could see ourselves in the vision for the march and for what followed.

That moment onstage—standing alongside two fierce women of color, fellow reproductive justice leaders Monica Simpson of SisterSong and Sung Yeon Choimorrow of the National Asian Pacific American Women's Forum, delivering remarks to a crowd that I later learned made up the largest single-day demonstration in U.S. history, declaring our steadfast and unwavering commitment to freedom—struck me as *historic*. I knew this march had sparked an upward trajectory of broad mobilization that will effectively and triumphantly change the landscape for all of us.

The next several years under the Trump/Pence administration are going to be hard. We've already witnessed atrocities. But let's be honest: The work has always been hard. We have survived years of struggles and injustices. We have always endured, strengthened by the resilience of our ancestors. We will press forward with deep fortitude and a clear, enduring vision of social justice, collective liberation, and love.

Washington, D.C.

Amy Schumer and Madonna
backstage in Washington, D.C.

MY WHOLE SELF, MARCHING

BY ELAINE
WELTEROTH

I'll be honest: I was skeptical about the march at first. I even debated whether or not to go. Perhaps it was the cloud of election defeat still hanging heavily over me, but I worried it would wind up being more symbolic than a mode of effecting any meaningful change. As a woman of color who has grappled more with what it means to be black in America than with the limitations (and unique advantages) of my womanhood, I have struggled at times with whether or not the feminist movement truly included me. Because race determines so much of one's daily lived experience with discrimination, my gender has always seemed secondary to my cultural identity. Don't get me wrong, I consider myself a woman's woman. But too often, I've felt alienated in white, female-centered spaces—the lone black woman left to explain why hashtagging "all lives matter" is indefensible or why asking to touch my hair is triggering.

Ultimately, I decided to march in D.C. anyway. I felt compelled to be part of what would surely be remembered as a historic moment and I opened myself up to experiencing it fully, even if it was just a big experiment within our own echo chamber, and even if it meant marching for and with women who only partially understood my plight.

Once I showed up, I was struck by how wonderfully intersectional the entire experience was. I witnessed all these different expressions of womanhood come together across divides of race, age, religion, status, and political leaning to make space for each other's voices. It was healing to see unity in diversity. I wasn't being asked to choose between being black and being a woman. People showed up as their whole selves: Muslim, queer, black, female—all aspects of their identity were celebrated.

I immediately realized I had miscalculated. I had underestimated the power of peaceful demonstrations at a time like this. Displays of solidarity go a long way in a world that's become as fractured as ours.

Elaine Welteroth is the editor-in-chief of *Teen Vogue*.

Just as Trump is credited with bringing out the worst in our country, in some ways the resistance has unearthed the very best in all of us. It's allowed us to see the humanity in one another and to stand with each other in our distinct struggles.

I went into the march questioning what purpose it served to band together with hundreds or thousands or millions of people who already agreed with each other that this presidency undermines democracy, human rights, and basic decency. But what I didn't account for was how much we all needed to feel connected as allies.

This feeling of intentional inclusivity that I picked up on was so clearly ingrained in the DNA of the event, part of the intention. Consider the speakers: MomsRising and the National Coalition on Black Civic Participation. The Council on American-Islamic Relations and Americans for Indian Opportunity. Planned Parenthood and Angela Davis. . . . It was such a meaningful display of how our stories and journeys are woven together into a narrative of what it means to be a woman in America and how we are stronger together. It sounds so cliché. Those clichés are why I almost chose to stay on the sidelines. But I'll never again underestimate the transformative power of women coming together. If the Women's March happens again, count me in.

Washington, D.C.

I, TOO AM AMERICA

Washington, D.C.

New York City

New York City

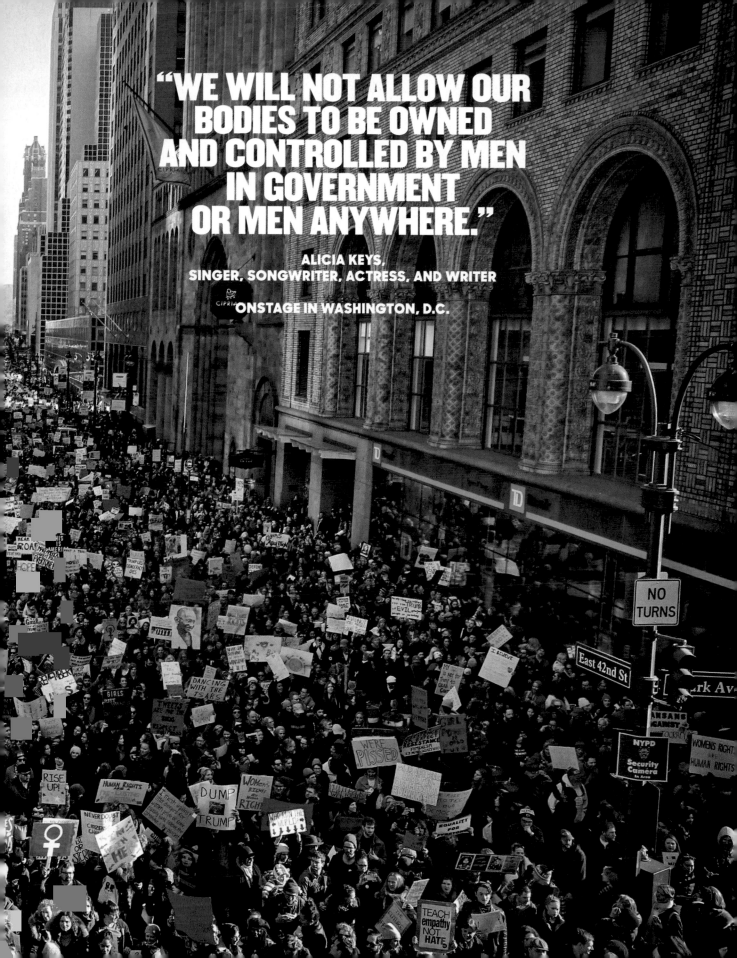

"WE WILL NOT ALLOW OUR BODIES TO BE OWNED AND CONTROLLED BY MEN IN GOVERNMENT OR MEN ANYWHERE."

ALICIA KEYS,
SINGER, SONGWRITER, ACTRESS, AND WRITER

ONSTAGE IN WASHINGTON, D.C.

Women march before organizing
a prayer circle in front of the
National Museum of the American
Indian on January 21, 2017.

LEAD WITH LOVE

BY JUDITH L∈BLANC

Judith LeBlanc, a member
of the Caddo Nation of
Oklahoma, is director of the
Native Organizers Alliance,
which trains social activists in
Indian country.

The Women's March remains, for me, a moment when I could exhale, because I saw that I'm not alone, that American Indians are not alone. At Standing Rock, we derived strength from continuing on the path our ancestors began. At the high point, 10,000 of us were bound together by a common belief in the power of prayer, our values, and being organized. Coming together showed the world we were willing to do whatever it took to protect Mother Earth and the sacred, not just for ourselves but for all of the people on the planet. The Women's March represented the same thing for those who marched. I felt compassion, reciprocity, and love. On that day, after Mothers of the Movement, the Fight for $15, and the Dreamers all took the stage and spoke, because of Standing Rock and the Dakota Access Pipeline, it was Native Americans' turn to stand up and show the militant strength of love.

Building a transformational movement is going to require us to take to the streets by the millions and to build community neighborhood by neighborhood and reservation by reservation. Every community out there—and we're doing it in Indian country—has to go deep and figure out what sacred organizing principles bring them together. Building trust and community on a one-on-one level is necessary in a moment when Trump uses the word *love* in order to spew hate and calls the people to come together on the basis of division. The only way we can break through that message is to take it down the old-fashioned way: by talking to each other. The Women's March was what all of us needed in order to remember that we are many and they are few, to remember that we are not alone, and that our community is very broad, very colorful, and all shapes and sizes. There is hope in that for me and, I think, for the millions of people who took to the streets on that day.

At Standing Rock, our love and commitment to the land, to our people, and to all the people of Mother Earth made us much stronger when we were facing rubber bullets, being hosed down, and watching drones flying overhead. It's harder in some ways to resist brutality with love, but it builds a core strength that can never be defeated. That's the kind of moral resistance people are yearning for. They're yearning for unity and a sense of humanity that will give us the strength necessary to survive very difficult conditions. If we're going to change the system, if we're going to have economic and racial justice, it's going to take resistance driven by compassion. There have been different moments in history when love was seen as a weakness, but, in fact, love and compassion are at the heart of what builds movements. They are at the heart of how our Indian people have survived.

There is now a battle between the culture of love, reciprocity, and compassion and the culture of division, hate, and fear. Only movements like the Women's March can intervene in that struggle, because when people truly see others, they recognize their humanity. My heart flew like an eagle to see so many young women marching. I believe they will remember that day for the rest of their lives, and they will refer to it as a day where they woke. They woke and realized that the only way forward is to be engaged. The only way forward is together.

THE WOMEN'S MARCH BY THE NUMBERS

200,000

Estimated number of actual marchers in Washington

Number of people march organizers expected to attend in Washington, D.C., January 21

800,000–1,200,000

653

Number of events that took place in the United States

13

Number of places in the United States that reported a march of one person. They are: Breen, Colorado; Chesapeake Bay, Maryland; Conover, Wisconsin; Crestone, Colorado; Evanston, Wyoming; Gila, New Mexico; Grants Pass, Oregon; Hildale, Utah; Mora, New Mexico; Pence, Wisconsin; Show Low, Arizona; West Lima, Wisconsin; Woods Hole, Massachusetts

2,200

Number of permit applications for buses bound for the Washington, D.C., Women's March

3,300,000

Number of people who marched on January 21 in the United States alone

5,000,000
Number of people who marched worldwide

Number of official Women's March T-shirts, designed pro bono by creative firm Big Monocle, sold via social-commerce platform Bonfire to defray operating costs of the Women's March

90,146

49
Temperature, in degrees Fahrenheit, at march time in Washington

-40
Temperature (with windchill) at march time in Unalakleet, Alaska, where some 40 people marched

444,786
Number of likes received by Hillary Clinton's tweet to marchers the morning of January 21: "Thanks for standing, speaking & marching for our values @womensmarch. Important as ever. I truly believe we're always Stronger Together."

150 Number of artists—among them Uzo Aduba and Zendaya—who joined the Women's March Artists' Table, committing to the mission, vision, and Unity Principles of the march

216

109,527

Number of marchers in the United Kingdom, which had the most marchers outside the United States

60,000

Number of pussy hat patterns downloaded before march day from pussyhatproject.com

5

Number of women who marched in a cancer ward at a Los Angeles area hospital

76

Age difference, in years, between the oldest and youngest speaker at the Washington, D.C., Women's March. (Gloria Steinem was 82; Sophie Cruz, the daughter of undocumented parents, was 6.)

2

Number of hours some D.C. Metro riders waited for trains to take them to the march

69

Population of Stanley, Idaho, where 30 people marched with musician Carole King (that's almost half the town!). She held a sign that said "One small voice," the title of her 1983 song about the power of one person to change the world.

3,014

Number of participants in an inclusive, online march organized by people facing physical limitations or chronic illness. At Disability-march.com, people could "march" via entries telling their story of why they joined the march online.

1,001,613

Station entries on Washington's Metro on January 21, the second busiest day in its history. (Barack Obama's 2009 presidential inauguration was the busiest; Donald Trump's resulted in approximately 571,000 rides.)

10,174

Distance, in miles, from Washington to the march that took place farthest from there: Melbourne, Australia, where up to 10,000 marchers hit the streets

Number of continents that hosted marches. (There was even a march in Antarctica! See page 66.)

7

2

Age of Women's March organizer Bob Bland's baby, in months, on march day. Bland's child was strapped to her chest as she addressed the crowd: "I had never done anything like this. You too can be an organizer."

More than 150,000 marchers gathered at Civic Center Park in Denver.

Brussels, Belgium

JAN 21, 2017 5:00 P.M. – MIDNIGHT

OWNING THE NIGHT

ALTHOUGH THE MARCH ENDED DURING THE DAY ON JANUARY 21, 2017, ITS AFTERSHOCKS REVERBERATED WORLDWIDE AFTER SUNDOWN. FROM 5 P.M. ONWARD, THE ORGANIZERS REFLECTED ON WHAT HAD JUST HAPPENED.

JANAYE   After the march, I remained on-site to watch as the march elements like the stage, sound towers, and other things were removed. I decided to walk to the Ellipse by myself to have a moment to take it all in. There were still so many women milling about as I walked, still gathering in solidarity. When I got to the Ellipse, there were women chanting and singing, placing their signs against the fence, and continuing the demonstration.

A few women came up to me and asked if I had been onstage, thanking me for the work we did to organize the event. In that moment of solitude and reflection, I realized that they might be tearing down the site where the march took place, but the feeling of solidarity and the united energy of women lifting up their collective voices would remain for a long time.

VANESSA   There were posters everywhere. I wish I had saved them! And women in pink hats celebrating. And a million parties—but none of them felt right to be at. While others were elated with what we had achieved, getting dressed up, celebrating, dancing, and so forth, I was sleepwalking through the motions. I felt—overwhelmed? Disassociated? I knew we had just begun—and acutely felt the weight of the work to come. I knew it would be formidable, and I knew it would be a lonelier journey. We would not always have 3 million friends out in the streets with us fighting this thing.

But later I recovered, and ended up being snuck in through the back door into the backstage of a club where all of our favorite comedians were performing in celebration of the march.

MIA   After having the flu for the entire week and no sleep the night before the event, I was dazed after the event. I couldn't even comprehend the number of people that attended or the amount of logistics we pulled off. My group of volunteers helped clean out the ADA tent and we donated all our supplies to the first responders who worked in a tent next to us. We hopped on the subway and I felt numb from exhaustion. I had to drive up to Annapolis, Maryland. When I arrived, my friends and family had food and drink already set up. Sitting there enjoying my first real meal of the day, I knew this day would be a flashbulb moment in my life. But at that moment, sitting at the dining room table, I was just happy to be celebrating the day with family and friends.

SARAH SOPHIE   Finally, late in the day, my daughter and I got to the Ellipse and we found Tabitha St. Bernard-Jacobs and her family. We walked together, feet aching, needing to pee, so hungry, back to the Watergate Hotel. We climbed into bed after promising each other to get out in an hour to go to the after-party, worried that if we didn't promise on it, we would be too tired. We ordered three orders of french fries from room service. When they came, the woman from room service saw my Women's March badge and, full of emotion, said, "Thank you. I saw you all leaving this morning and wanted to join. But I'd be fired. I was marching with you in spirit today." And, OK, I cried again. And hugged her.

Washington, D.C.

MEREDITH My daughter and I made our way to a restaurant filled with women still wearing their pink hats celebrating. The TVs at the bar were filled with coverage of the marches and we had the best-tasting burger and milk shake I think I have ever had.

TED I had been the first person on-site the night before the march, so when it was over I was truly a withered, wet, and crumpled fall leaf. My pain meds I take for two disabilities had worn off, and all I wanted to do was sit. But the excitement and energy of the day fueled me to rove around looking for food, water, and a restroom. I settled for a Diet Coke and Cheetos from CVS on a park bench. People were everywhere and it made me smile; it seemed like newcomers were still falling like a waterfall down Independence Avenue toward the main stage. Finally, I grabbed my cane and walked two stations down to catch the Metro.

It was solid packed, and honestly my body was about to give out even though my heart was still full. Right then a woman from Ohio saw the national organizer badge I was still wearing and my cane. She yelled to her friends and they parted the way for me to get into the train. I will forever be grateful for their kindness.

JENNA After the march, traffic from D.C. to New York was such a bitch. And lo and behold, it's raining, bumper-to-bumper, but every car has a

---

"YOU COULD SEE SOLIDARITY IN EVERYONE'S EYES."

JOANIE: I'm the author of a series of nonfiction books about my father's WWII-era life as a forcibly displaced person after the Nazis occupied his Czech homeland. During the 2016 election cycle, the vitriol among the presidential candidates, primarily Mr. Trump's verbal attacks aimed at various religions, races, immigrants and refugees, women, the LGBT community, and the disabled reminded me eerily of the subject matter I was researching for my books: Nazi Germany in the 1930s. The night of the election, my daughter Kelly called me, sobbing. She was sorrowful for America and for her children having to live in what appeared to be a mean-spirited and unjust America. When she heard about the march, we knew we would go—along with her daughter Ava, my son Derick, and his wife, Carol.

CAROL: By midafternoon on November 9, I realized I would be part of the resistance and registered with a march group on Facebook. I let my husband know of my plans and told him that I'd welcome his company but understood if he preferred to sit this one out. He decided to come along and coordinated to meet up with Joanie and the rest of our family. I was born in Brazil and am a U.S. citizen now, and I work in international business development, so it doesn't take a lot of convincing for me to pick up a torch. At the march I was so fascinated by the excellent organization and execution of this huge event, which taught me so much about intersectional feminism. Everything about the march felt so overwhelmingly positive. You could see solidarity in everyone's eyes. Even when we were flipping the bird as we marched in front of Trump's hotel, we were positive and upbeat. I never felt hungry, thirsty, or tired all day. The demonstration provided all the nourishment I needed.

AVA: As we rode the train into D.C. from Baltimore the morning of the march, my "Meemaw" Joanie posted on Facebook about heading into the march. She looked at her phone with a frown and showed us a comment a Facebook friend had left. "How is your privileged life suffering in this great democracy so that you need to go to the march?" I asked if I could write the reply. I typed this out: "Why does my life have to be bad to join the march? Why can't I stick up for those people who need help in some way but often don't have the opportunities to use their voice to speak up? We are here to speak for them." The march was a memory I'll take with me throughout my life.

KELLY: I heard how many people might attend the march, but I was a skeptic, especially because the media predictions about the election were so screwed up. But I was glad to be going with my family. When we arrived at 5:30 A.M. it was eerily quiet. We secured a spot near the video screens and waited as the crowd swelled by the minute and eventually engulfed the Mall. We literally didn't move for six hours because you couldn't. While it was an electric atmosphere, I was also sort of afraid. I thought, What is my exit strategy? How will I get out of here if something happens? My daughter is next to me; how will I protect her? I had no cell service the entire time we were watching the speakers and singers, so I had no outside perspective on what was happening. It was like we were in a massive bubble. Once we made it outside of the main march area, I called my husband in Orlando. He was elated. He said, "Honey, have you seen the television? The crowds are incredible! Los Angeles, Paris, London, New York, Atlanta, everywhere—you just made history!"

THE SCHIRM FAMILY
Joanie Holzer Schirm, 68, Orlando, author; Carol Incarnacao-Schirm, 32, New York City, senior business developer manager; Ava Lafferman, 15, Orlando, student; Kelly Lafferman, 47, Orlando, CMO; marched in Washington, D.C.

THERE WAS BLOOD
OUT OF HER EYES, BL
OUT OF HER W

MUST BE A PRETTY PICTURE
YOU DROPPING
TO YOUR KNEES

A PERSON WHO IS
FLAT-CHESTED
IS VERY HARD TO BE A 10

DISGUSTING
ANIMAL

E WAS BLOOD COMING
T HER EYES, BLOOD COMING
OF HER WHEREVER

×80

A JOUR
A JOURN
PIECE OF

DISGUSTIN
ANIMAL

Washington, D.C.

Washington, D.C.

protest sign or someone wearing a pussy hat or something like that. I remember thinking about the day, tears just streaming down my face, trying to process it. And then the operator in me started going: Well, wait a second. Where's all of our data? How are we recording all of this stuff? How are we keeping track of all these names?

EMMA   A lot of the women that I helped organize in Florida were from rural areas. I love my Miami group. I love the West Palm group. I love the Key West group. They're great. But what really, really makes me happy is the Saint Augustine group and the Jacksonville group. Because that's not where you typically think of women rising up and sharing their voices in the South.

As we were planning the march, we had these rural southern and Midwest groups that met in these rural places, and maybe it would be just four or five of them. They'd be in these small towns, and they never really talked about politics before, and now, all of a sudden, these groups of five or six women are meeting at diners in their pink pussy hats. And that's their own little resistance. They got in the car, and they got up to the march, and now since the march, at a very minimum, they keep meeting at the diner in their pink pussy hats and they write their postcards and they call their senators. And it doesn't always have to be a loud, million-person march to have an effect, right? It's sort of the whole you-drop-a-stone-in-the-pond-but-the-ripples-keep-reverberating thing.

"I AM MY ANCESTORS' DREAM. THEY FOUGHT FOR ME TO BE ABLE TO STAND UP HERE IN THE COLD-ASS SNOW IN FRONT OF A BUNCH OF WHITE PEOPLE WEARING UGGS."

**JESSICA WILLIAMS,
ACTRESS AND COMEDIAN**

ONSTAGE IN PARK CITY, UTAH

Congresswoman Maxine
Waters, Cher, Teresa Younger,
Congresswoman Barbara Lee,
and Congresswoman Brenda
Lawrence in Washington, D.C.

Washington, D.C.

WE WILL NEVER STOP FIGHTING for what's RIGHT

CLOSING THE GAP

BY
CONGRESSWOMAN
MAXINE WATERS

U.S. representative Maxine
Waters has represented
California in the House
of Representatives since
1991 and has served on
the Democratic National
Committee since 1980.

Backstage, before I spoke at the Women's March in Washington, my mind went immediately to the many marches I've been involved in during my lifetime. I couldn't help but reflect on the work of fellow activists in my past, people like Gloria Steinem, Bella Abzug, and so many others. I met up with Gloria backstage and my heart fluttered to see her, and we embraced and talked about old times.

But I will be honest: I was also feeling as if there had been a long gap. So much time had passed between when we had been together on those marches, what we had accomplished, and today. I had really begun to think that the women's movement was lost, that younger women didn't appreciate what we had done, and why. I thought they were more focused on their careers, thinking that a women's movement didn't enhance their opportunity for upward mobility, that they didn't want to be aligned with it. They didn't think they needed it.

I lined up to speak, and I could not believe what I saw. I had heard there would be 250,000 people present; it was more like a million. It was unlike any march I'd been to before. For one thing, there were the pink hats everywhere. The signs were the most creative that I have ever seen. And the women who had organized the march had included people of all cultures and backgrounds in their leadership and planning.

Going in, I had been feeling disappointed, even a bit resentful, toward the younger generation. I was under the impression that they thought what we had done for women's rights wasn't important. But seeing the size and passion of the crowd and realizing that the younger women there recognized what we had done and that they were carrying our torch made me realize I'd been completely wrong. And as I left the stage and marched with groups of young women, I saw that they did know the history. Some of them even recognized me and called out my name, and it was thrilling to me to connect with the younger generation. We walked from the stage all the way to the White House and I was in a state of euphoria. It was a wonderful, wonderful experience.

Los Angeles

AFTER

Washington, D.C.

JAN 28, 2017

FROM MARCH TO MOVEMENT

WITH THREE TIMES AS MANY ATTENDEES IN WASHINGTON AS TRUMP'S INAUGURATION, THE RECORD-BREAKING GLOBAL WOMEN'S MARCH WAS SO POWERFUL THAT IT DEFIED ITS ORGANIZERS' EXPECTATIONS, AND THE MEDIA TOOK NOTE. THE PINK PUSSY HAT APPEARED ON THE COVER OF *TIME* MAGAZINE, WOMEN'S MARCH STORIES TRENDED ON SOCIAL MEDIA, AND ARTISTS EVOKED THE DEMONSTRATION IN VIRAL IMAGERY LIKE MAINE PAINTER ABIGAIL GRAY SWARTZ'S RENDERING OF A BLACK ROSIE THE RIVETER ON THE COVER OF *THE NEW YORKER*. THE WOMEN'S MARCH TEAM QUICKLY BEGAN TO DISCUSS HOW TO LEVERAGE THE MOMENTUM THEY HAD IGNITED.

BREANNE   About nine days after the march were the airport protests against the Muslim ban. President Trump had suspended entry into the U.S. of people from seven countries, six of them Muslim-majority. As hundreds of travelers were detained, the protests began. This was something so spontaneous that we didn't have anything to do with it, obviously.

LINDA   My role is to use my social media platform to effectively disseminate information, and it was no different for the airport protests. They were mostly ad hoc—people showed up and it gave me so much hope immediately after the Women's March. These protests were what I needed to see as a Muslim American, that my fellow Americans had our back.

ALYSSA   The airport protest was the first victory of the resistance. The Women's March was important as a symbol of resistance, but it wasn't a win in the sense of changing policy. The airport protests made a tangible impact. Showing up really does make a difference, and the airport protests were the first time we saw that happen. Not to mention the sheer magnitude of that day. There wasn't one body calling for airport protests. Everyone had the same idea and it spread by social media. The Women's March platforms used Facebook Live throughout the day to bring the protests to everyone, even those who didn't live near an airport.

VANESSA   Of course, the groundwork of the resistance has been laid for years, but I think what we did was we made it mainstream and really gave people an easy on-ramp to stand up and start saying, "You know, I've got to do something personally about this." And I do think that we changed the world in that way. We changed history. I think that the airport protests, and people coming out en masse after that, are examples of what we jump-started and what people now refer to as the resistance.

SARAH SOPHIE   A lot of people say that the airport protests wouldn't have happened without the Women's March, but what I like to remind people of is that the Women's March wouldn't have happened without all the amazing organizing of Black Lives Matter. BLM was training the American people to go out on the streets and stay out on the streets for years before the Women's March came about.

MARIAM   I woke up that morning at my parents' home on Long Island with plans to catch up with a good friend from high school. But I was following the news about the travel/Muslim ban and texting with Alyssa and knew that I had to do something. I called a friend and told her we needed to cancel our plans and go protest at JFK. I didn't think she'd be into the idea, but she immediately agreed! Now, to add some context, Tori had never attended a protest, not even a Women's March. But I think the realization was dawning on everyone that our values were at stake and we didn't have any option but to mobilize.

   Both of my parents are immigrants from Afghanistan and escaped war. The life they've built here for me and my two younger sisters is the epitome of the American dream, and Trump's victory was a wake-

up call that a very real racist barrier was going up against the beauty and possibility of this dream. The essence of the dream that my father believed in 30-some-odd years ago, that allowed him to build a life for himself and his family and that gives hope to millions of people around the world, was being snatched away. We had—and have—no other choice but to organize against this hate.

SOPHIE We really just kind of leapt into action. There was no shortage of catastrophes to respond to from the minute he became president. I was live-tweeting what was happening at JFK, asking folks at airports from around the country to send us updates of what was happening in their cities.

PAOLA Tamika, Carmen, Linda, Janaye, and I were all together at a conference in Los Angeles when people started just showing up at the airports. So we all went to LAX, and what we saw was so amazing. It was so beautiful and inspiring to see so many people organizing spontaneously for communities that were not their own. This was the whole point and the purpose of the Women's March—to show people, to tell people that we

Linda Sarsour and protesters
at the #NoBan rally.

Muslims pray as supporters gather at Los Angeles airport on January 29, 2017.

had to organize not just to protect ourselves, but to protect the most vulnerable communities around us. And in this case, the most vulnerable communities were and are the Muslim community, the undocumented community, the LGBTQ community, and the black community.

MRINALINI I get questioned regularly about why as an immigrant I fight for a country that is not mine. I always respond: "Not only is this country mine, but, more importantly, its people are my people, and it is for them that I fight. I embraced America, its people, its culture, in all their glory and their shortcomings, with open arms, and never sought to 'integrate' myself into American society. Rather, I focus daily on celebrating my roots while cherishing the positive values that drew me to this country. I keep my voice loud and refuse to be a bystander while people like me, and those much more marginalized than me, are targeted. My love and belief in this nation drives me to fight for my vision: that no nation is inherently great; its people have to be committed to a continuous struggle to make it a little bit better each day than it was the day before."

Los Angeles airport protesters.

"I'M HERE BECAUSE I AM A WOMAN. BUT I'M ALSO HERE BECAUSE I AM A BLACK WOMAN. AND I'M HERE BECAUSE I'M A MUSLIM WOMAN."

**ILHAN OMAR,
MINNESOTA STATE REPRESENTATIVE**

ONSTAGE IN ST. PAUL, MINNESOTA

GETTING POLITICAL . . . WHEN YOU CAN'T VOTE

BY YARA SHAHIDI

It was 7 A.M. on Tuesday, November 8, 2016, and I was a sixteen-year-old at the polls, tagging along to vote, vicariously, through my parents. Although I was two years away from voting age leading up to the election, I had given my time to various Clinton campaign initiatives to encourage youth participation, doing my best to fulfill my democratic duty.

Flash forward to 12:01 A.M. November 9, 2016: The unbelievable results were in, and I couldn't even process a result that I thought could only occur in an alternate universe. I thought, *What would the outcome have been if all of my voting-age friends had participated in the election?* A sense of helplessness came over me but I knew that feeling helpless wouldn't do any good. Instead, I began to dig deep and find other ways in which I could actively participate in our democracy. Coming from a family of activists, I have seen firsthand the infinite power that "We the people" possess to inspire true change. I had to recycle this negative energy I was feeling. I needed positive momentum.

And then the Women's March happened: Positive momentum in a moment where I felt as though no one cared about equity, about the people whose very presence was endangered by the new administration. The Women's March proved that *we care*. Regardless of gender, ethnicity, race, or class, *we care*. I was lucky enough to attend the Los Angeles march with my mama and my TV mama (Tracee Ellis Ross), where I was surrounded by love, inspiration, and action. I bumped into friends, other activists and artists that I look up to, all there for the same reason, for closure, so that we could start anew. Being onstage, looking out into the unending crowd, the sea of people reminded me that there is no end to those of us who are dedicated to taking action, and loving one another amidst the chaos. I doubled down on my resolve to continue to participate. I know that I can gather a group of people and I can commit to myself and my community and continue fighting for what I believe in.

My takeaway from the Women's March? Even if, like me, you are not of voting age, there are so may things that we can do, like calling our elected officials, or continuing conversations with family members about issues that are important to us, to move our country in a compassionate, inclusive direction. We may not yet have the ability to vote, but we do have the power to influence the vote.

Yara Shahidi, activist, actress, and philanthropist, stars in *Black-ish*.

Washington, D.C.

BY KATERI
AKIWENZIE-DAMM

MY OWN
MARCH

I am a single mother of two beautiful, caring Anishinaabe boys and the guardian of another boy with severe neurological challenges. We live in a small house in the Chippewas of Nawash Unceded First Nation at Neyaashiinigmiing, in Ontario, Canada. Living here is a purposeful choice on my part. As an older mom, and the mom of adopted children, I decided to do everything I could to ensure that my sons would be known and loved by our community. I want them to know they have a homeland and culture that can sustain them when life's dark clouds gather. I was supported in this way as an Anishinaabe child, and it gave me an inner strength I've drawn on repeatedly throughout my life.

When I was younger, I was active in indigenous youth politics. At university I yearned for, but couldn't find, courses about indigenous issues. Instead, I found courses on women's issues. But even as I took part in marches and protests, much of the feminism I encountered seemed very white, urban, middle-class, and empowered in ways that I knew many of us were not. How could I relate? I read, for example, that women in Canada got the vote in 1918. But First Nations people in Canada weren't able to vote until 1960. So-called women's suffrage in Canada excluded First Nations women—we weren't considered worthy. Indigenous women have lived under a different set of laws, survived a different history, and experienced a different reality than nonindigenous women in Canada. The rights and recognition we've won we've had to fight for as indigenous people.

When I learned after the U.S. presidential election that so many white women had voted for Donald Trump despite his blatant racism and misogyny, I wasn't surprised. In a society that privileges whiteness, there's protection in being white. The same goes in Thunder Bay, Ontario, today, where white women don't have to worry about their children being found drowned in the river or about walking down the street and being mortally wounded when a trailer hitch is thrown out of a car at them by a young man who triumphantly yells, "I got one!" This is

Kateri Akiwenzie-Damm,
a spoken-word artist, writer,
and editor, is the founder
of Kegedonce Press, a literary
publishing house devoted
to indigenous writers.

what happens to First Nations people here. But the racism that feeds it feeds violence against indigenous women all over Canada and the U.S.

Nor was I surprised when I heard that a Women's March was being organized to protest the new U.S. president; after all, he's absurdly vocal about his misogyny. But I was wary. Who were the organizers? Who would be included? Obviously, the thought of women, children, and men rising up to show the Trumps of the world that they would fight against misogyny was exciting. But it wasn't enough—I wanted the march to fight Trump's hatred of LGBTQ people, Mexicans, immigrants, Muslims, and indigenous people. Because if a women's march isn't about making real change for indigenous women, trans women, immigrant women, Mexican women, black women, Muslim women, it's not a "women's" march. As one of the signs held during the march in Vancouver said: "Feminism without intersectionality is just white supremacy."

As the planning for the march progressed, it was, in fact, designed to incorporate a wide range of voices, including indigenous women. I saw photos from marches across North America of indigenous women in turquoise scarves, fists held high, holding handmade signs, drumming, singing, and wearing traditional clothing. It was beautiful. Deep down, though, I dreamed the marchers would use their collective power to support the peaceful indigenous protesters and their allies at Standing Rock who were suffering incredible violence from police, corporate goons, and local racists. That kind of activism didn't happen. There were postings on Twitter in support of #NoDAPL and Standing Rock, which increase awareness. But when people's civil rights are being trampled day after day for months, are a few tweets the most we can hope for? We need real-world actions to back up those words. I'd hoped that the Women's March would be a catalyst that would bring more women to stand shoulder to shoulder with indigenous women, not only at Standing Rock but in places like Thunder Bay and wherever we march or dance or put our lives on the line to end violence and oppression.

We can't, in Canada, or anywhere in the world, pretend that the misogyny and racism out in the streets in the United States are not also where we live. We can't pretend that we aren't connected. After what happened at Standing Rock, no one should be surprised by what took place in Charlottesville.

I wanted to be at the Women's March, just as I had wanted to be at Standing Rock. Instead, like many others who are caregivers, single parents, or without the support and resources to travel, I followed Standing Rock and the Women's March online while I did my best to parent my sons in a way that helps them to reach their full potential as the loving, happy, healthy Anishinaabe they are meant to be. This is the most meaningful act(ivism) of my life. When they are older, I'll be back out there, sign held high, raising my voice, using my presence once again to send a message against hate, injustice, and destruction. And my sons will be there with me, supporting, protecting, and standing strong in our fight for justice and love.

Washington, D.C.

Washington, D.C.

BY DAVID REMNICK

AMERICA THE EXCEPTIONAL

Protest is thrilling. Protest can rattle established ideas and unnerve existing structures. It can inspire solidarity in the protesters and provoke ideas far beyond the field of demonstration. Protest can thrust forward heroic leaders who articulate and embody models of rhetoric, valor, and endurance. In the face of injustice, protest is the assertion of humanity and will, a demonstration that there is a point at which a woman or a man will not concede, will not bow down. As Virginia Woolf, the unlikely radical of Bloomsbury, put it, "The voice of protest is the voice of another and an ancient civilization which seems to have bred in us the instinct to enjoy and fight rather than to suffer and understand."

And yet. As invaluable as peaceful protest can be—the other kind almost invariably backfires—it's what comes next that counts. Tahrir Square was thrilling. The fires! The songs! But it ended with the rise of the Muslim Brotherhood and then, after another round, with more or less the same military dictatorship they started with. From Mubarak to Sisi in no time flat. At the cost of being reductive, much the same can be said of the mass demonstrations in Tehran, Bahrain, Moscow, Minsk, Beijing, Tashkent . . . Since 1989, democratic protests have made the streets vibrate with liberated cries of self-assertion, but in so many cases the process ended, quickly or over time, with blood, with restoration, with the reassertion of authoritarian politics. The number of democracies around the globe rose—then fell, just as fast.

And that is where we are in the United States. Donald Trump, who disdains constitutional norms, was elected President appealing to the lowest urges and praising global authoritarians: Putin in Russia, Erdogan in Turkey, Sisi in Egypt, Duterte in the Philippines. In Saudi Arabia, he was no doubt delighted to see the order on the streets—the utter lack of visible dissent. Scorn is an emotion he saves for the European Union and NATO.

In his inaugural address, Trump envisioned an end to American generosity; it was a cri de coeur of white nationalism, Charles Lindbergh

David Remnick is editor of *The New Yorker*.

taking the oath of office. The marches that followed on January 21 were, in national sum, the greatest mass protest in the history of this country. Which was, and remains, thrilling. It was proof that millions of people would not relent in their commitment to the Constitution, to human and civil rights, to their sense of self-possession and good humor, to their humanity.

We Americans are exceptionally lucky in ways we are usually too beclouded to recognize. We are not cursed with an authoritarian history, a weak constitution, and repressive forces lurking in every corner. We are blessed with a history (however darkened by slavery and other injustices) and institutions (however plagued by mediocrity) that hold out the promise of democratic struggle, of politics. Politics that hopes to fulfill, incrementally or suddenly, the hopes of protest. Politics that seeks, through civil argument and the often ugly process of lawmaking, compromise and new realities. That is the struggle. Resistance is not

THE MARCH WAS PROOF THAT MILLIONS OF PEOPLE WOULD NOT RELENT IN THEIR COMMITMENT TO THE CONSTITUTION, TO HUMAN AND CIVIL RIGHTS.

merely marching and protest; it is citizenship; it's the doctor, the teacher, the reporter, the factory worker, the councilperson, the parent . . . all of us doing what we can to ensure that Donald Trump is an episode and not a permanent condition.

On the fiftieth anniversary of Bloody Sunday, the great clash of nonviolent civil rights protesters and their armed nemeses as they tried to march from Selma to Montgomery, President Obama gave a speech on this theme in Alabama. Selma is sacred ground for the birth of voting rights (a right that is once more endangered) and for civil rights. In places like Selma, people bled to demonstrate their commitment to democratic politics, to civil rights and basic decency.

"We know America is what we make of it," Obama said. "We are Sojourner Truth and Fannie Lou Hamer, women who could do as much as any man and then some; and we're Susan B. Anthony, who shook the system until the law reflected that truth. That's our character. We're the immigrants who stowed away on ships to reach these shores, the huddled masses yearning to breathe free—Holocaust survivors, Soviet defectors, the Lost Boys of Sudan. We are the hopeful strivers who cross the Rio Grande because they want their kids to know a better life. That's how we came to be.

"We're the slaves who built the White House and the economy of the South. We're the ranch hands and cowboys who opened the West, and countless laborers who laid rail, and raised skyscrapers, and organized for workers' rights. We're the fresh-faced GIs who fought to liberate a continent, and we're the Tuskegee Airmen, Navajo code-talkers, and Japanese Americans who fought for this country even as their own liberty had been denied. We're the firefighters who rushed into those buildings on 9/11, and the volunteers who signed up to fight in Afghanistan and Iraq. We are the gay Americans whose blood ran on the streets of San Francisco and New York, just as blood ran down this bridge."

If there is such a thing as American exceptionalism, that's a good description.

The way to right wrongs is to turn the light of truth upon them.
—Ida B. Wells

A Day Without a Woman protest on New York City's Fifth Avenue.

MAR 8, 2017

A DAY WITHOUT A WOMAN

TWO WEEKS AFTER THE MARCH, THE ORGANIZERS MET TO DISCUSS THEIR GOALS MOVING FORWARD, THEN UNVEILED A PLAN TO ORGANIZE A GLOBAL STRIKE ON MARCH 8, INTERNATIONAL WOMEN'S DAY. IT WOULD BE A ONE-DAY DEMONSTRATION OF ECONOMIC SOLIDARITY IN WHICH WOMEN AND THEIR ALLIES WOULD TAKE THE DAY OFF FROM PAID AND UNPAID LABOR, AVOID SHOPPING EXCEPT AT SMALL, WOMEN- AND MINORITY-OWNED BUSINESSES, AND WEAR RED—ALL TO SHOW SOLIDARITY WITH THE CAUSE. THE IDEA IGNITED SUPPORT *AND* CONTROVERSY IN BOTH PROGRESSIVE AND CONSERVATIVE SPACES.

MY BODY
MY CHOICE ♀
MY C♥UNTRY
MY V👄ICE
#ADA#

A Day Without a Woman
in New York City

Silence = Violence

A DAY WITHOUT A WOMAN

MEREDITH   We decided to reconvene after the march. It was a chance to reflect, celebrate, and express gratitude, and a chance to strategize and organize. I was thrilled to bring two skilled and incredibly effective facilitators to guide the weekend's discussions, B. Cole and René Redwood. We had come together to work on a moment, and now we needed to plan for a movement.

PAOLA   We went to our retreat at the Omega Institute in Rhinebeck, New York, and it was Janaye and Tamika who had said that they wanted to do a general strike. So I asked, "How does this fit into the frame of the Women's March?" So we debated—there were probably like 50 of us—we were all debating around what does that look like, how do we do it. There was a woman, Julianne Hoffenberg who is part of The Justice League NYC, and she said, "Why don't we do A Day Without a Woman, similar to *A Day Without a Mexican*? The movie, right?"

We all jumped on that, and were like, Yes, that's brilliant. We started organizing and it was our first major action after the Women's March.

CASSADY   I come from a labor-organizing background. I grew up very low income. This idea of a general strike felt so radical, like a reach-for-the-stars kind of thing. We got all kinds of ignorant comments on it—"Oh, well, strikes are only for privileged women." But the only strikes that have ever been effective are the ones by people who were not privileged.

For me, it's not so much about whether A Day Without a Woman was a success in terms of numbers or things like that. I think it was a really big deal to be putting this radical messaging out there. The power of the people to collectively strike and withdraw their labor from the system for a day was really rocking the boat. I hope that it laid a lot of groundwork, especially for young people who will see this as something viable, a power-building tactic.

TABITHA   A Day Without a Woman was geared toward working women, but young people and teenagers got pretty involved. A lot of them found it shocking; they couldn't believe that women still get paid less than men.

SARAH SOPHIE   When we were planning A Day Without a Woman, the organizers who are mothers were like, "We have to talk about emotional and gendered labor. We have to talk about caregiving and unpaid labor and all the things that we do for free, and the amount of hand-holding and coaxing and cajoling of the male ego we have to do." You can't account for emotional labor in money terms, but it's this uncompensated work that lets the patriarchy flourish. The amount of energy that women have to expend— and I'm a very privileged woman, so my level is much lower than most women's. But all of those things really became even more clear.

ALYSSA   A Day Without a Woman was a test for the Women's March, a test of whether we could keep it up and this wasn't just a one-shot event that was going to be over in a few months. We weren't sure it would work.

"I'M FIGHTING FOR THE RIGHT FOR A WOMAN TO BE JUDGED ON THE CONTENT OF HER CHARACTER VERSUS HER SHAPE IN A SKIRT."

TAYLOR SCHILLING, ACTRESS

ONSTAGE IN NEW YORK CITY

TAMIKA There were numerous internal conversations about whether we could really get people to sacrifice and potentially risk their future by not going to work or protesting in a place that may not be welcoming. But when I saw the number of people who showed up for New York City's Day Without a Woman, I said, "OK, this thing is going to work."

GINNY Seeing support from major media companies—from Condé Nast and MTV going red to the Netflix video in support of the day—it reinforced that we are on the right side of history; that standing up for women is standing up for true equity and a value placed on human rights and women's rights. I was arrested that day, for civil disobedience, but for me it was a statement—I was standing up for all the marginalized and disenfranchised women in this country. Historically women have been silenced. Guess what? We will be heard.

CARMEN I was walking by Central Park with Cassady, heading to the New York City rally, and ahead of us I saw a group of eight women dressed in red and laughing as they crossed the street. One called out, "Hey—can you take a picture of us?" They were office coworkers taking their break together as a symbolic walkout. They had no idea who we were, but they saw the red we had on too and started talking about how much A Day Without a Woman meant to them!

MICHAEL And then the fact that people around the country participated and that members of the Women's March team got arrested in New York and told the story of how they were willing to give up their bodies for the movement—it was amazing. If you go back to the great Harry Belafonte, to Diane Nash, to Ella Baker, and you talk to them about what made the movement, they'll say, "You've got to give your body."

PAOLA And then we got arrested. It was—it was all over the news. But that moment of arrest was very spontaneous. We hadn't planned it out. It was Linda, Tamika, Carmen, myself, Ginny, Alyssa, Sophie, Cassady, Faiza N. Ali, Breanne, Bob, Chantal Felice, and Sasha Ahuja.

Ginny Suss, Tabitha St. Bernard-Jacobs, Paola Mendoza, Linda Sarsour, Carmen Perez, Bob Bland, and Breanne Butler march on A Day Without a Woman.

TABITHA A group of us organizers were marching to Trump Tower from the A Day Without a Woman rally. When we neared Trump Tower, we linked arms and veered right into the middle of the street. As the police started to demand that we get off the street, we dropped to the ground with arms linked and occupied the middle of the intersection. The police swarmed around in an instant and started to yell for us to get up. We continued chanting with linked arms. The police gave warnings to get up or we would get arrested, right before they started pulling women up by their arms and arresting them. It was complete chaos.

LINDA First of all, it was not an orchestrated arrest. Let's be clear about that. We were not expecting to ask women to take a day off of work so that they could spend a day in jail. But it happened. Thirteen of us that day got arrested. And then there we were, sitting for like eight, nine hours in a jail cell. And it was beautiful. We were singing freedom songs. It was another transformative moment, of building sisterhood and solidarity with the women who were there, who were mostly, except maybe one, officially part of the Women's March.

Shianne Norman, a mother who lost her four-year-old child to gun violence, speaks at A Day Without a Woman in New York City.

GINNY It was very quick. They arrested us within five minutes. And they put us in the wagon, but we were very joyous in the sense that we were able to do some civil disobedience around this idea of what it means to have a day without a woman.

MICHAEL They sat in the middle of that road and people from around the world saw these courageous women getting arrested. Now one of them happened to be Paola, so I thought to myself, "This is amazing, but shit, what are Mateo and I going to do to help?" And Mateo saw a photograph of Paola in handcuffs, and he said, "Why is Mommy in handcuffs? I thought police are nice."

And I said, "Mommy got arrested today because Mommy's protesting."

He said, "We've got to go get her out." And I said, "OK." He said, "I've got to put on my Power Ranger costume." So he put his costume on. We picked up some sushi just in case we were going to be there for a while. And we headed down to the precinct and waited for her to come out of jail, until late in the evening, and him in his Power Ranger outfit.

TABITHA Once everyone was arrested, I headed to the jail with a group of other Women's March people and waited there for the next five hours.

BOB I had my baby Chloe all wrapped up and with me at our morning rally. When we started marching I handed her to Kim Russell, a gun violence survivor and grassroots organizer. And thank goodness I did, because less than an hour later, we were arrested. I was apprehensive but grateful to know that Chloe would be taken care of, whether or not I was able to reach out and let Kim know what happened.

CASSADY Getting arrested was like the biggest privilege walk I could take. It made me think of Kalief Browder and Sandra Bland and all the black and brown people who are arrested for things that I, a white woman, would not be arrested for; who don't have a team of loved ones singing songs in the cells around them, gathered in front of the precinct, and

---

MY MARCH

"HOW COULD I PREDICT HOW MANY HATS WOULD BE THERE?"

As soon as I heard of the march, I knew immediately I'd go to D.C. But I wanted to do more. What sign could I hold up? What could I wear? I wanted my actions to have meaning.

As an L.A. girl, I knew I'd be cold in January in D.C. I'd recently become obsessed with knitting. I was riding in the back of my parents' car when it clicked: Maybe I could knit my own hat. And if *I* can do it, anyone can. Suddenly I could see a whole sea of pink hats—an aerial view—in my mind's eye. I wanted to do cat ears, but I was worried they'd be too hard. I asked my knitting teacher what to do, and—lo and behold—cat ears are the easiest to make.

We launched right after Thanksgiving. The press covered it. It was all over social media. People were learning to knit just to make a pussy hat. But as much as I believed in myself, there was a level of suspense. How could I predict how many hats would be there on march day?

On Saturday I woke up at 4 A.M. A friend and I had 5,000 hats to pass out and we put them all in Ziplocs and then in trash bags. At one point, we were trudging with the heavy bags across the Mall, and a woman in an SUV made an illegal U-turn. "Are those *pussy hats*? Can I help?"

All of a sudden, we got to higher ground and I could see all the way down the Mall. It was all pink. Oh. It hit me. I was in a dream state. My friend said, "You have to take this in. *This worked.*"

I arrived at the march tired of feminism that's telling me to play by rules that I didn't agree to. I felt like I'd been playing this rigged game, like Cinderella: The patriarchy tells you, "As long as you finish all your chores and wear a beautiful dress, you can go to the ball." At first that sounds reasonable. But Hillary did all her chores, and she was presentable. The patriarchy never intended to let Hillary go to the ball.

The pussy hat has gotten criticism, but that's fine with me. It represented something greater than a pink hat. The pussy hat shows you're not alone.

KRISTA SUH
29, Los Angeles, artist and writer;
marched in Washington, D.C.

WATCH

During the arrest at A Day
Without a Woman.

sending prayers from afar. Getting arrested was a privileged activity for me. But when the privileged people intentionally enter a system that isn't designed for us, we disrupt the bigger system of making some people worth more than others to begin with.

PAOLA   I was put in a cell with Linda and Faiza, who organizes a lot with Linda. And we were talking around what we could do around the Muslim ban—we were in the cell for like six hours. We wanted to do something that was not just a march; something where art and activism collide. So we came up with this idea to make a human banner that would say #NoBan, and we pulled it off. There were like 10 inches of snow on the ground—and we found a park and Mikhael Tara Garver organized it all within three days; about 300 people showed up. We made a human banner that said #NoBan over this beautiful white snow. And we got a drone to photograph it, and it went viral. It was amazing and beautiful.

LINDA The #NoBan action happened because the women who were in jail weren't just looking at that day, we were looking ahead, and at ways to show solidarity to other communities. I am very grateful that my Women's March sisters have always showed up for my community, in ways that are really transformative. And I think many of them would have shown up in the past, if they had a relationship with a Muslim. I feel like my participation in the Women's March opened up for them a whole new community that they now feel like they're in solidarity with.

MY MARCH

"IT'S JUST A MATTER OF TIME BEFORE WE TAKE POWER."

I had doubts about Hillary's ability to win, but people said it was going to be OK. At church, my pastor said, "Jesus has got this." My daughter was 16, working on Hillary's campaign and harassing me to join her, so I did voter registration on Election Day. But when the returns came in, I felt sick. We had some friends over, and everyone went home early. I cried. I grew up in the sixties when everything was changing and there was a lot of hope. Now we're almost having to fight those old battles all over again. But we're not going back.

Then I read about the Women's March. I knew I didn't want to be in Washington when all those Trump people were going to be there for the inauguration. I had been at both of the inaugurations for Obama, and going when Trump was there would be horrifying. So I decided to go to the Cincinnati march. In Cincinnati, you don't know what you're going to get—Ohio is pretty conservative—but it was a lot of people. I ran into a student who's in my Constitutional Law course. He said, "Professor Williams? You're here!?" I said, "Of course I'm here." The crowd was diverse. Not just white women. Women of color. LGBTQ people. Signs about reproductive rights. We were all speaking out against the horror that was this election. We were saying, "This is not the country we want. This is not the leader we want. This is not who we are." We were chanting, "People united will never be defeated!"

When I got home and saw on Facebook and Twitter that women had marched all over the world, it was overwhelming. Later, scrolling through Twitter, I realized there were people in Antarctica marching! When you compare the march to people who turned out for Trump, there were more of us. And it's just a matter of time before we take power. I'm getting goose bumps.

VERNA WILLIAMS
56, Cincinnati, Ohio, law professor;
marched in Cincinnati

...because MOST WOMEN Can't Leave Work Today

A Day Without a Woman in New York City.

March organizers Mariam Ehrari, Jasmine Blackmon, Tabitha St. Bernard-Jacobs, and Sarah Sophie Flicker at A Day Without a Woman.

"I STAND HERE AS A QUEER BLACK TRANSGENDER WOMAN FROM AUGUSTA, GEORGIA. BUT I AM ALSO A DAUGHTER, A SISTER, AN AUNTIE, A FRIEND, A LOVER, A HUMAN, A FEMINIST."

RAQUEL WILLIS,
NATIONAL ORGANIZER, TRANSGENDER LAW CENTER

ONSTAGE IN WASHINGTON, D.C.

BY ILANA GLAZER

YOU ARE HERE

The Women's March in Washington smelled cold, like brisk fall, even though it was January—evidence for the Resistance that science is real and so is global warming. It tasted like the Eastern Mediterranean cuisine by a Spanish American immigrant chef at Zaytinya, which was packed with fellow peaceful protesters giddy with pride and kinship. It felt like the rumble of the Lincoln Theatre during the 2 Dope Queens show I guest-hosted with Phoebe Robinson, one of my best friends and my chosen sister. Stand-ups like Michelle Buteau and Tig Notaro talked about their tig-o'-bitties and how to politely respond to being misgendered, respectively. The march sounded like chants and songs, the key to keeping a large group of people sane, focused, motivated. It looked like a sea of different kinds of people, every kind of person you could imagine—hot people, not-hot people, angry millennials and over-it baby boomers, children who were so excited to be there and believe most deeply in the cause, gay kids and old gay folks, black people, people in wheelchairs, brown folks and traditional heteros "all fired up, ready to go."

These were some of my favorite chants from the march, and gosh, does it feel good to remember them:

"Hands too small/Can't build a wall," referring to 45's tiny, weak hands and the administration's proposal of building a literal wall to separate Mexico and the U.S.

"Fuck Mike Pence; Fuck Mike Pence." A simple four-four rhythm that gets the gut. It was started by a bunch of young, hetero white boys. Yas/LOL.

One of my favorite signs said "My wife is a Muslim and not a terrorist, but I'm scared of her anyway." First of all: LOL. Second of all: That is some advanced LOLs we're enjoying over here . . .

Another winner: "Shanté, we stay," a send-up of RuPaul's quote from *Drag Race*: "Shanté, you stay." Ru paved the way for so many people, and there we were, walking that path.

But the saddest yet most effective sign of all was "Women's rights

Ilana Glazer is a writer and performer in New York City. She is best known for cocreating *Broad City*.

are human rights," a famous Hillary Rodham Clinton quote from the 1995 Fourth World Conference on Women in Beijing, 22 years earlier.

The white people were angry. Really, really angry. I grew up in a small, conservative town in Long Island in the nineties; it was nothin' but white people pretending everything was AMAZING. Twenty years later, I had never seen so many angry, progressive white people. They felt backed by the people in the streets, protected by those around us. White people were screaming about equal rights for black lives, ashamed of their white privilege, ashamed that it took till now to scream about that inequity.

Men of all ethnicities and orientations were singing, yelling, shouting all day, ready to share their privilege without fear of losing it, ready to advocate for women and complete the cycle of progress. White women were recognizing the distinction between white feminism and intersectional feminism. And we all realized we had been taking science and fact for

THERE'S NO FULL-THROTTLE, ZERO-TO-100 WOKENESS. THERE ARE LEVELS OF WOKENESS THAT YOU KEEP PEELING AWAY AND UNCOVERING OVER TIME.

granted and that even these things necessitated our explicit support.

There's no shame in not having it all figured out. One's sense of self develops over a lifetime, so you can't actually have it all figured out until the moment before you die. Just keep reading, talking it out, and learning from mistakes. There's no full-throttle, zero-to-100 wokeness. There are levels of wokeness that you keep peeling away and uncovering over time. At the march, I saw people all along their individual journeys, from babies and toddlers to Gloria Steinem.

We marched and chanted, walking slowly as one single, global organism, 5 million people connected through space and time. We had the world stage. Progressive thought entered the mainstream social consciousness and acquired a greater visibility and deeper validity. We made noise that was impossible to ignore and rerouted our nation's narrative. Our movement was big enough to represent the "average American" for a day. Well, actually a whole weekend. We were too many to ignore and we're growing. Watch out for us—there's more to come.

Florence, Italy

WOMAN'S RIGHTS ARE HUMAN RIGHTS

Oakland, California

BY JIA TOLENTINO

THE BEAUTY AND THE DANGER OF THE WOMEN'S MARCH

From the beginning, the greatest thrill of the Women's March has been tied up with the thing about it that most disquieted me. Throughout the buildup to the demonstration, during that wild day of collective avowal, and now, increasingly, in the months that have followed, it has seemed very likely that the Women's March would be a once-in-a-lifetime event.

In one respect, of course, it had to be! It needed to be the greatest political demonstration that any of us had ever seen. We should thank whatever mercy still exists in this increasingly entropic universe that the Trump presidency—already a catastrophic era to anyone with a conscience—began with a day like January 21, with its massive global efflorescence of knit hats and homemade signs. The Women's March needed to be, and was, an aberration on par with Donald Trump's election. We had to outstrip even *his* preposterous capacity for spectacle. Every person in that grand, motley, proud, and humble coalition was necessary to create that shot to the heart, that dazzling inoculation, whose effects have been slowly fading as the punishing year grinds on.

For some significant portion of its participants, the Women's March will be, I suspect, the alpha and omega of extracurricular political action—and by that I mean the beginning and end. Again, this was the most beautiful thing about it and also the scariest: That day felt like a window of delicate, stunning possibility that would close at sundown and never open as wide again. In the lead-up to the demonstration, I realized how many people I knew who considered themselves progressive had always assumed—nearly all of these people being white and middle-class or richer—that the government would, without requiring their active attention, work in support of them.

In practice, in effect, that was all they cared about. In theory, of course, they may have cared about everyone and everything, but we should let go of the idea that good intentions lead directly to justice. Mine certainly haven't. These days I keep returning to Martin Luther King Jr.'s polite excoriation, in "Letter from a Birmingham Jail," of the white

Jia Tolentino is a staff writer at *The New Yorker*.

moderate who "prefers a negative peace which is the absence of tension to a positive peace which is the presence of justice." He wrote, "Shallow understanding from people of good will is more frustrating than absolute misunderstanding from people of ill will."

To get specific here: Trump's election seemed like the first time many white women realized—*really* realized—that America is often unfair and heartless. (A shocking number of nominally liberal white men, of course, have yet to take this fact to heart.) The generosity of the Women's March lay in the way the demonstration transformed and assimilated the sudden thirst for justice expressed by confused and vividly affronted members of the straight, white middle class into concrete, intersectional action. Their concerns became fundamental to this enormous marching coalition, voiced alongside fears and angers that were much older, sharper, more immanent, rooted more deeply. On that day, our causes, our concerns, our fears, our safety, and our future seemed intertwined.

But if the beauty of the Women's March was in its mass

THE PRESSURE THE WOMEN'S MARCH EXERTED MADE IT CLEAR THAT WE EITHER GO OUT OF OUR WAY FOR EQUALITY OR COUNT OURSELVES IN THE WRONG.

acknowledgment of interdependence, it scared me to remember that this basically came at the pleasure of white people. The tricky thing about interdependence is that people with power can deny it indefinitely and whenever they want. Every marginalized group in America knows that its fate is bound up with the political positions of white people, but—to understate things—it does not come as easily to white people to grasp that their fate is bound up with others. I have started to feel that white people *have* to be responsible for our country's necessary revolution. (In the tragedy in Charlottesville and the massive subsequent demonstrations, white people have shouldered this responsibility to staggering ends.) Trump's platform is, in so many ways, theirs to undermine. Sixty-three percent of white men and 53 percent of white women voted for Trump. In the Women's March, we saw how meaningfully the remainder of white people—white women, specifically—can leverage their position. The things middle-class white women support are quickly clothed in acceptability; whatever they care about can approach the mainstream.

During the Women's March, we all picked up concerns beyond our person. Asian families carried Black Lives Matter signs. Men chanted for reproductive freedom. White families cheered against deportation. It was stunning to me to see so many straight, middle-class white women who had possibly imagined the single worst problem in America to be the abortion rights rollback—i.e., the travesty that most directly affected them—absorb with great openness that mass incarceration, anti-LGBTQ discrimination, racist policing, and the erosion of worker protections posed a long standing and immediate threat to their peers.

Since the march, a remarkable number of white women have thrown their weight behind the moral truth of interdependence, campaigning to save DACA or fight anti-Muslim travel bans. Many have grasped it more clearly but nonetheless slipped back into that familiar state of inert, well-meaning concern. Some portion, I suspect, never really got it, and imagined that day, without even consciously thinking so, that black people were marching for black issues, immigrants for immigrants, and all the white women marching for their own. This faction will not go out of their way again unless they are the center of attention. And I wonder too if some white women are so accustomed to being centered that they believed, on January 21, simply because of the name of the demonstration, that everyone was out there marching in support of them.

Since the Women's March, in trying to navigate the space between hope and brutal disappointment, I have tried to expect everything from people and require nothing of them at the same time. Yes, that window of social possibility will never open so wide again, but it isn't closed yet. Every day we can replicate the pressure the Women's March exerted, which made it clear that we either go out of our way for equality or count ourselves in the wrong. We did all this, of course, on the wrong side of a terrible moment in history. But if the Women's March showed that lateness is generally a sign of some tragedy, it also showed that it's never too late.

CAN SOCIAL MEDIA CHANGE THE WORLD?

FROM THE INCEPTION OF THE WOMEN'S MARCH PLANNING PROCESS, THE REVOLUTION WAS AND WILL CONTINUE TO BE TWEETED, FACEBOOKED, AND INSTAGRAMMED.

ALYSSA I'm very happy to go on record saying that Trump's tweeting a typo, "covfefe," one night in May was the shining moment of the resistance for me. My response tweet, "Cause Only Very Fragile Egos Fear Equality," was probably the easiest tweet that I've ever written. So it's kind of a funny story. I saw "covfefe" trending, but this was like the one time I didn't click to see what the story was. I was being a little lazy that night.

And then Sarah Sophie texted me and was like, "Going to bed, but Covfefe, you have to look at it. It's amazing." So I looked and I thought, Why don't we create an acronym? I think it took like 30 seconds of thinking of words. I texted it over to our social media deputy Sophie, and I was just missing the last *E*. And she came up with the *E* and then we put it out. And I think it was like our most impactful tweet to date. This was a moment of realizing the power of art in the resistance. And I think that social media is one of the key platforms for that. One of the things that I'm proudest of from my work is our sign-of-resistance series that we do on social media. Each day, we pick a different sign of resistance, which is just resistance-related art, and we put it up on Women's March Instagram, Twitter, Facebook. A lot of the artists that we spotlight are young women of color and other marginalized groups. For me it's the coolest thing. I'm continuously blown away by seeing the work that artists are contributing to the resistance.

PAOLA A similar thing had happened back in April with #DropOReilly. It was eleven o'clock at night, and I saw that BMW was not going to be advertising on Bill O'Reilly's show anymore after it was reported that he had paid settlement charges over sexual harassment accusations. I texted with Alyssa and a few others, saying that we should start a new campaign trying to get O'Reilly fired. And everyone was like, Yes, yes, yes, let's do it, let's do it. So Alyssa and I thought around the hashtag, and she came up with #DropOReilly. The next morning I woke up thinking, What we need to do is we need to have women share their stories around sexual harassment. We put out that call, and #DropOReilly was inundated with women sharing their stories of sexual harassment in the workplace, and they ranged from being inappropriately touched to sexual assault. Thousands of stories were shared as the hashtag trended. Again, this is where we bring activism and art together, because essentially what we're doing, what we were doing in that moment with our social media, was storytelling. We were having people engage and tell their stories, and it's in the telling of stories that you get to change people's hearts. You get to

"WE NEED TO PUT THE ACTIVE INTO OUR ACTIVISM."

CHRISTINE LAHTI, ACTRESS AND FILMMAKER

ONSTAGE IN LOS ANGELES

Organizers get good news from the public relations team's Janna Pea (left).

The Resistance Revival Chorus performs at a protest.

change the idea and perception of what it means to be or do something. And we've taken that same concept to various issues.

We did the same thing with #HowTheACASavedMyLife, where we had people share their stories around how the Affordable Care Act had saved their lives. These stories were heartbreaking and beautiful, and I've organized a lot around health care, so this was a very personal issue for me. Within three days of launching, that hashtag had over 150 million impressions on Twitter alone. I remember reading those stories and literally I would cry. There was this one story of a little boy who was born with heart problems, just like my little sister. His mom found out he was sick while she was pregnant. His first surgery was over $200,000, and if the ACA didn't exist he would never have been able to have gotten health insurance, because his heart problems were a preexisting condition. And without health insurance he wouldn't have been able to get the surgery that saved his life.

ALYSSA Where Women's March plays a role in the bigger picture is to take concepts in activism and organizing and to make them as accessible as possible to the entire country. What we wanted to do was make intersectionality understandable for everyone and take this scholarly concept and make it part of everything that all of us do, not just parts of the population—at least everyone who believes in fighting for the greater good. That was something we started before the march and we've continued to do since.

SARAH SOPHIE Another gem from Mr. B was when he said, "Sometimes you gotta preach to the choir if you want them to keep on singing." When we feel tired or overwhelmed I think about this—that we have to restore our own force in order to keep on going. I realized this movement needs music, old protest songs, new protest songs! So a group of us formed the Resistance Revival Chorus: me, Ginny, Paola, Alyssa, along with Nelini Stamp and Shruti Ganguly. We now have 60-plus women singing together because we know that joy is an act of resistance! We created a tool kit so people in other states can form their own choruses too.

MY MARCH

"I'M PAINFULLY AWARE OF HOW LITTLE POLITICAL AGENCY I HAVE HERE."

I was willing to spend a night in jail in Singapore. That was the worst-case scenario when I thought of demonstrating in solidarity with the Women's March. But realistically, the actual worst case would also affect my partner, Nick. At stake would be my "Dependant Pass"—God, those words—and Nick's Employment Pass, which are the keys to our life as Americans in Singapore.

Somehow, that's the worst kind of suppression of speech. Not only do I not have any rights to speech or assembly here, but my actions aren't even my own. Moving here from Massachusetts in 2015, I didn't expect to feel the impact of this chilling self-censoring. Since the election, I'm painfully aware of how little political agency I have here in Singapore.

There are very limited ways for anyone to demonstrate here, and all involve permits. Sister events organized for January 21 were limited to letter-writing campaigns and a cocktail hour to raise money for women's groups. The latter was sponsored by a company called Vanilla Luxury, which sounds like the translation for "white privilege." Could we not do something more than post a few letters or console ourselves over a martini?

I wanted desperately to be a part of the historic moment. I wanted to be seen and counted. I wanted to wear my "The Future Is Female" T-shirt. It never happened. People showed up publicly on every continent—in Antarctica! But not in Singapore. I had never felt more disenfranchised than I did on Women's March day. But friends back home reminded me that the real fight is in the actions that we can take, with our voices, with our resources, and with our time.

Time zones ahead of D.C., I showed up in the only spot I hoped to find any action, the Speakers' Corner in Hong Lim Park. Aside from a tourist taking a selfie, and a gardening uncle I suspected might be patrolling the place, it was empty. I took my own selfie, my small act of feminist defiance. Later on Facebook I saw a Singaporean woman had the same idea and showed up in the same place. I would have spotted her by her pink pussy hat.

I couldn't use my body, but I will use my voice in any way I can.

SARA M. WATSON
31, technology writer, Singapore; "marched" in Singapore

BY SENATOR TAMMY
DUCKWORTH

DO SOMETHING

In many ways, being at the Women's March reminded me of President Obama's first inauguration, in 2009. That day, everyone was packed together, miserably cold but also hopeful and joyful and grateful to be a part of history. There was so much optimism in that inauguration crowd; people were excited about what the next few years could bring. I was thinking about that at the Women's March, when I was again part of one of the biggest and most unified crowds I have ever seen—except this time, there was an undercurrent of fear but also a determination to make a difference.

Driven by worry about what the next few years could bring, people turned out in droves. I brought my daughter Abigail, who was a little over two at the time. I keep a picture of my husband and me holding Abigail at the march on my desk. It was her first protest. I wanted to bring her, not only so she could get a taste of what it means to be an active, engaged citizen but also because the march was about the future, and her generation will be impacted.

After the 2016 election, so many people came up to me and said my victory in the Senate race was a rare shining light on election night. Many would give me hugs and many even started weeping on my shoulder. This happened for weeks. I felt like a counselor whose job it was to provide words of encouragement, though I, too, felt like all of our rights were under threat.

At the march, I thought about how our country needs women to step up and make an impact, now as much as ever. So when I got up to speak, I told the crowd: The best way we can fight for our rights is for more people to get involved in the political process. Stand up and make your voice heard. Don't just let the march be an experience that you post about on Facebook. Let it be a starting point, the beginning of you doing something meaningful.

As I travel my state, I make the same ask: Do something! Run for office or for student council. Join the board of a nonprofit, or become

Tammy Duckworth is a retired U.S. Army lieutenant colonel who has represented Illinois in Congress since 2013, first as a member of the House and since January 2017 as a senator.

a member of a local Women's March chapter. Try to mentor women in other parts of the state where there aren't Women's March organizations. My Illinois colleague, Representative Cheri Bustos, has started a training program called Build the Bench to train candidates for office. It's a great idea. In politics and in life, you never know what you can achieve until you try.

Since the march, I've noticed how people are more willing to step up and fight for what's right without being asked. When the President tried to implement his first Muslim ban, crowds of people quickly showed up at local airports to support travelers who were detained by the Department of Homeland Security. People started demanding their representatives hold town halls. They flooded the phone lines in congressional offices and showed up at events to counter KKK demonstrators and neo-Nazis. Everywhere I turn, people are becoming more active as they grow outraged by what is happening and how our

SINCE THE MARCH, I'VE NOTICED HOW PEOPLE ARE MORE WILLING TO STEP UP AND FIGHT FOR WHAT'S RIGHT WITHOUT BEING ASKED.

nation's values are being betrayed. America is finally awake, and I think it started with the march. We have to keep that momentum up and not let it fade as we get further and further from January 2017.

When I think about how we can hold on to that activism and keep people engaged, I think about what it means for my little girl. Before the election, I had been looking forward to a night that would cement her rights to fair pay, to a safe workplace environment, and to make decisions about her own body when she is older. And all of that is in peril right now. We have to remember that, hold on tight, and fight for our rights.

A statue of Eleanor Roosevelt in New York City's Riverside Park.

WE ARE THE
ONES WE HAVE
BEEN WAITING FOR

Washington, D.C.

NAVY M

FALL 2017

"RECLAIMING OUR TIME"

CONGRESSWOMAN MAXINE WATERS MADE THE PHRASE "RECLAIMING MY TIME" FAMOUS AS SHE REPEATEDLY INVOKED IT WHEN HER QUESTIONS WERE DODGED AT A HOUSE COMMITTEE MEETING. THE WOMEN'S MARCH TEAM WOULD INCORPORATE HER WORDS (WITH HER BLESSING) AS AN OFFICIAL THEME FOR THEIR WOMEN'S CONVENTION HELD IN DETROIT IN LATE OCTOBER. THE GOAL: TO BRING THOUSANDS OF NEW ACTIVISTS TOGETHER TO TAP INTO THE POWER OF WOMEN AS A FORCE FOR CHANGE. ON THE EVE OF THE CONVENTION, WOMEN'S MARCH ORGANIZERS REFLECTED ON THE IMPACT OF THE MARCH AND HOW THEY WERE MOVING FORWARD.

LINDA   Detroit is a city with historical and political significance. Many of the issues that led us to march in January 2017 are happening in Detroit and surrounding areas: economic inequality, environmental injustice, de facto segregation, ICE raids, violent policing, and overall unequal access and opportunity. At the same time, nearby Dearborn is a city with the largest Muslim population in the U.S. And Detroit is home to a long and radical history of grassroots activism. Just like our movement, Detroit cannot be compartmentalized.

MEREDITH   The thing I've been most struck by since the march is how many people I've heard say, "I've never done anything like this before." But the march gave an entrée into the movement. It was like an easy service road onto the highway. I think that was really striking.

TAMIKA   I believe that the Women's March will go down in history as an incubator. So many women who got involved had not been engaged in social action before, including many people in leadership roles. And they got a very crash course. They got educated quickly on issues that they had been ignoring or they just didn't know existed, for whatever reason.

White supremacy and misogyny is in the fabric of the country. We needed people to see and understand that. Since the march, we've seen a lot of women get active, get out there, and say, "I'm sorry that I didn't know what you were dealing with, but I'm here now. I want to be in the movement." For some, it moved them to a place of action. But I also think that there is something to be said about a greater level of consciousness, for women who were directly involved in the march and for women who just attended or watched from the periphery.

SOPHIE   We do represent a mainstream feminist movement, even though I don't think our politics are mainstream. But we are mainstream because we are widely known and have large-scale participation.

GLORIA   I've heard people say they measure their lives as before or after the march. The danger is symbolized by Trump in the White House—the triumph of a hierarchical minority with the nuclear code, plus a fear that a newly emerging majority power of diverse women plus men of color will treat the Trumps of the world as they have treated others. This could be lethal. The upside is that the majority of us are now aware of the danger, the interdependence of our movements and issues, and our massive, bottom-up power. We are woke!

And in all kinds of ways. For instance, this march made visible and personal the line between what might once have been seen as separate issues. Racism can't be maintained in the long run without controlling reproduction—which means controlling women's bodies—so there is no such thing as being feminist without also being antiracist, and vice versa.

DE'ARA   This goes in particular for the black women who came out, who always historically come out: How do we figure out how to leverage our political power? Yes, absolutely I want more women to be pro-choice, I want

Three of the Women's March cochairs—Tamika Mallory, Carmen Perez, and Linda Sarsour—in Washington, D.C.

"ALL OUR SONS ARE IN HEAVEN AND WE CONTINUE TO FIGHT FOR OUR CHILDREN. . . . WE ARE GOING TO CONTINUE TO FIGHT. WE'VE COME TOO FAR TO TURN BACK NOW."

SYBRINA FULTON,
MOTHER OF TRAYVON MARTIN

ONSTAGE IN WASHINGTON, D.C.

Actress Alia Shawkat at the Women's March in Washington , D.C.

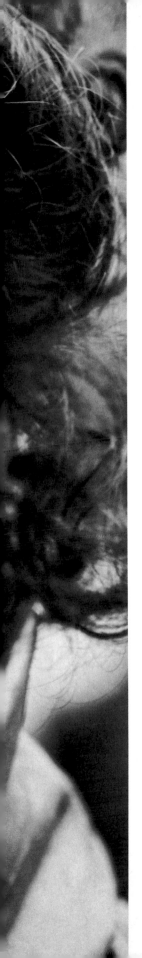

more women of color elected. But while we're working on that, how do we hold our party accountable right now to the women that we currently have in office, and how do we leverage that power so that in the next presidential campaign, the black women on that campaign don't have to scream and shout to get the resources that they need? How do we make sure that in our national campaign people of color are being hired in leadership positions and that they don't feel marginalized?

GLORIA   The march spirit taught us we all have power from the bottom up in how we vote, how we spend our dollars, how we raise our children, how we treat each other, what we choose to say, and when we choose to march, lobby, or run for office ourselves.

MARIAM   After the march, it was evident that the Women's March was the beginning of a movement. We established a 501(c)3 and 501(c)4, nonprofits focused on issue education and political advocacy, respectively. Oftentimes, as it has become the nature of the beast, we have to be reactive. But we've been building to ensure proactivity too, as these issues came long before Trump—he has just given them more of a platform.

Our added value in the space right now is making sure our base understands the importance of how working on and showing up for issues they previously didn't realize they should show up for will impact how people vote in the 2018 and 2020 cycles. Little did I know the Women's March would become an organization. But we're a force!

BOB   Some of our greatest organizers to this day came on at the very beginning, within the first few hours of organizing the march, when none of us knew each other and we were all total strangers. Most of us were also total beginners, so the other lesson I learned is it's OK to be new at something. It's OK to start fresh and trust in your innate wisdom. Women are resourceful, women are generous, and together, women can do anything.

CARMEN   What I see is young girls finally being able to read history books that have women who look like them. I want to see women standing in their power to fight against xenophobia, homophobia, mass incarceration. . . . I envision there being a woman president. The fact that the Women's March was a catalyst for so many is a testament. I feel women will change not only the political landscape but the cultural landscape of this country.

TABITHA   I often get emails from young people who want to get more involved in politics and in organizing. That makes me hopeful for the future of the movement because they will be taking over at some point and they are so ready.

CASSADY   I hope that women who care deeply about reproductive rights and equal pay will become as active for racial justice, immigrant rights, trans inclusivity—and learn to confront our privilege in those spaces. I think that is what can make our leadership—women's leadership—the transformative force we need in our society, if we include everyone at the decision-making table.

MY MARCH

"WOMEN KEPT APPROACHING GLORIA STEINEM TO THANK HER, AND THEY WOULD BEGIN TO CRY."

Before the march I considered myself an activist but more as a philanthropist, supporting events to raise money for the causes I cared about. I was very focused on supporting women and girls' education in other countries, but this election and the march made me realize I needed to be just as supportive of the issues right here at home. When we got to D.C., I was shocked by the number of people there—those who marched in wheelchairs especially inspired me.

Weary and exhausted after a full day of marching, my friends and I boarded the train back to New Jersey the following day. We arrived at our seats—which were four seats surrounding a table—and there was already one person seated there, Gloria Steinem! We could not believe it. Gloria was incredibly humble and gracious, speaking with us for most of the two-and-a-half-hour trip home. Even though she's 82 years old, she felt like my contemporary—casually dropping the "f-bomb" in conversation. I couldn't help but start to cry as we spoke. My friends and I kept thanking her for all that she's done for women, but she immediately thanked us right back for marching and told us she was just lucky that fighting for equal rights was her job. We fell into conversations about the value of stay-at-home mothers, equal pay, abortion rights, and, of course, Trump.

I texted my mom from the train to tell her we were sitting with Gloria. Mom asked me to give her a hug and I did. My friend took a photo and I laugh at it now because I just couldn't help crying, even during the photo. I wasn't alone, though. All during the train ride, women kept approaching Gloria to thank her and they would begin to cry. I'm so grateful we had this incredible experience—I'll never forget the most surprising thing Gloria said to us: that women will always have to fight for their reproductive freedom. Because of that, since the march, I've joined a group that regularly writes to our representatives about the issues most important to us, like abortion rights, education, and gun control.

MELISSA BAKER
46, Summit, New Jersey, restaurant owner; marched in Washington, D.C.

EMMA   There are women running for the school board all the way up to the federal government. And that's incredible. For me, I'm running for state government, for Florida State House. And I think a lot of it is this: The march happened, and what folks don't get is that we were all volunteers. You know [*laughs*], we signed up—the national teams that laughed at me, I have and still do have a full-time job throughout all of this.

Can you imagine that kind of work ethic in our legislature, that kind of single-minded passion because we're not doing it for fame or fortune, we're doing it because we truly believe in a better tomorrow, and that it will be affected by our actions?

A lot of people ask me if I would have run if Women's March hadn't happened. Maybe. My background is in policy. I've worked in unions. I've worked in not-for-profits. So maybe it was going to come. I don't know that I would have felt the sense of confidence or urgency or the ability to say, "Well, hey, I decided on a whim that it was the right thing to do to throw the biggest march in history. Why can't I shoot for the stars and run for office and effect change in a Republican-

Washington, D.C.

led state? Of course I can." And I think a lot of women are feeling that way since the march.

SARAH SOPHIE We may have lost the opportunity for the first woman president, we may momentarily have lost our country, but in the process we found our soul, our unified vision, and, more personally, our family.

PAOLA The resistance is made up of radicals, moderates, first-time organizers, Bernie Bros, and Hillary lovers. We have been inspired by the disability community being arrested for their right to health care. Our hearts filled with hope when 40,000 people marched in Boston against white supremacy. We have been stirred to action by young people risking deportation so they can stay with their families in the only country they have ever known. Imagine what we would be able to do if we had all the believers, all the dreamers, all the fighters with us, organizing, voting, and running for office.

GLORIA The future depends not only on the elections of 2018 and 2020 but on what we do each day between then and now. I hope we spend less time asking "What should I do?" and more time saying "I'm going to do whatever I can."

"HE DOESN'T HAVE TO MAKE AMERICA GREAT AGAIN. AMERICA IS GREAT. IT'S THE GREATEST COUNTRY IN THE WORLD, AND BECAUSE OF ALL OF US."

MAYOR MARTY WALSH

ONSTAGE IN BOSTON

LINDA   The only way for us to win is by organizing together, which means having critical conversations around racial justice. We may lose together. But I would rather lose with dignity and principle than throw any other movement under the bus. Because inevitably, we will win together.

AfTER THE STАrT

BY ROXANE GAY

Roxane Gay is the author of the *New York Times* best-seller *Bad Feminist*, a professor at Purdue University, and a *New York Times* op-ed contributor. Her latest book is *Hunger*.

I did not march in the Women's March on January 21, 2017. I had a long-scheduled event I could not cancel so I actually spent most of the march on an airplane, following march-related events around the world on Twitter. Women, men, and children from all walks of life contributed to a remarkable show of force in the face of the American disgrace that was the election of Donald Trump as president. The sheer number of women participating in so many cities great and small overwhelmed and inspired me. I was unexpectedly moved, and for the first time since the election, I felt a little bit hopeful. The march was messy and imperfect, but it was a meaningful display of what might be possible if women, if people, could come together in a sustained and ongoing way.

I had a prior obligation, but I also had misgivings about the march. Like many black women and other women of color, I had complicated feelings about the march, how it began, and how this newfound solidarity was so long in coming. It took something as drastic as the election of a white supremacist to motivate women, en masse, to march in such a powerful demonstration of unity and repudiation. Somehow, the mass incarceration of black men, the state-sanctioned murders of black men and women by law enforcement, the pay gap between white women and women of color, the health care disparities between white women and women of color, and so many other issues were not drastic enough to inspire the kind of outrage seen in the months up to and during the Women's March. That was and is disheartening.

Fifty-three percent of white women and a staggering 62 percent of white women without college degrees voted for Donald Trump; they were more interested in protecting whiteness than womanhood. Nearly a year after the fact, I remain stunned by these statistics. Perhaps, instead of marching, white women should have had frank conversations with each other about what a vote for Donald Trump truly meant for so many marginalized people—the working class, the LGBTQ community, people of color, immigrants, the Muslim community, people with disabilities, undocumented Americans—people whose lives suddenly became infinitely more precarious on November 9, 2016.

My initial concerns about the Women's March are largely the same issues that have always surrounded mainstream feminism. Any movement in support of women has to recognize that women have complex identities. Women are not affected equally by the ways of the world. As Dr. Kimberlé Crenshaw put it, "Different things make different women vulnerable." Intersectional feminism, a term coined by Crenshaw, accommodates this complexity, but not all feminism is intersectional. Certainly, as the march evolved into what it became, the agenda did reflect intersectional values, codified by the Unity Principles. It was a good start.

The march also presented a significant challenge. What happens after that good start? In the coming months and years, we have to find the best ways to sustain the energy and enthusiasm generated by the Women's March. It is relatively easy to show up for one day. How do we show up not just in historic moments but in our everyday lives, in our

HOW DO WE FIGHT FOR OURSELVES WHILE ALSO FIGHTING FOR THE GREATER GOOD? HOW DO WE HOLD OURSELVES ACCOUNTABLE?

own homes and communities? How do we keep fighting when it feels hopeless to face an incompetent administration, a self-serving and inept congressional body, and a justice system that rarely demonstrates a concern for actual justice? How do we fight for ourselves while also fighting for the greater good? How do we hold ourselves accountable and force ourselves to make the difficult, inconvenient choices that will be demanded of us? How do we take up the fight when some of us are simply too weary to continue the fight alone?

I don't have answers to these questions, but I know we need to find a way to be imperfect and messy but committed to making sure that what happened in November 2016 never happens again. The Women's March was a good start, but it was only a start.

Washington, D.C.

Washington, D.C.

BY VALARIE KAUR

REVOLUTIONARY LOVE IS THE CALL OF OUR TIMES

On election night, the future had never felt darker. Each hate crime, incitement to violence, and deadly proposal during the election season had hurt me from the inside. As a new mother to a little brown boy, I had to confront a painful truth: My generation of activism had not made the nation safer for my son. The last time I remember being in so much pain was on the birthing table. I began to ask a question: *What if this darkness is not the darkness of the tomb but the darkness of the womb?*

I got my answer on the day of the Women's March, when I carried my two-year-old son in my arms into the streets of Los Angeles. We became part of one roaring river of music and longing, grief and outrage, defiance and joy. All day, friends sent me photos of women across the U.S. and around the world holding up signs that answered my question: *This is the darkness of the womb*. We were birthing something new. Millions were choosing life over death in one collective breath.

Then it began: the onslaught of executive orders, Muslim bans, border walls, pipelines, budget cuts, and hate crimes harming the most vulnerable among us, including my Sikh community. We have barely had a chance to breathe between the crises. But my own family's century-long history here reminds me that white supremacy, nationalism, and racism are as old as the U.S. In 1913, my grandfather sailed from India to California, where immigration officers took one look at the turban he wore as part of his Sikh faith and threw him behind bars. He would have been deported if it were not for a white lawyer who fought for his release. My grandfather became a farmer in California's Central Valley. Years later, when his Japanese American neighbors were rounded up in concentration camps during World War II, he looked after their farms while they were away; their grandchildren still farm that land today. White supremacy is as old as America. But so are acts of revolutionary love—and every act of love inspires another. Policy wins alone will not solve the conditions that gave rise to this presidency. We need a new public ethic to birth a new future, a public ethic of revolutionary love.

Valarie Kaur is a movement lawyer, award-winning filmmaker, and founder of the Revolutionary Love Project.

As a lawyer, I have cringed at the word *love*. American culture too often mistakes love for the delirious rush of oxytocin that marks the experience of falling in love. If this is our only definition, then of course love is too fickle, sentimental, and ephemeral to be a political force. But after I became a mother, I saw love with new eyes. Love as mothering is a form of sweet labor that transforms and births anew. Love is not any one emotion but employs many emotions in that labor: Joy is the gift of love. Grief is the price of love. Anger is the force that protects it.

Historically, the labor of love has been confined to the domestic sphere. Yet spiritual geniuses from Buddha to Jesus, Muhammad to Guru Nanak, called us to practice love beyond family and tribe. Social justice leaders from Gandhi to King to Day grounded their movements in love to free the oppressed without hating the oppressor. Such love disrupts the status quo, confronts injustice, and shifts collective consciousness. The Women's March was a declaration of love.

Revolutionary love—love for others, opponents, and ourselves—is the call of our times. Loving only ourselves is escapism, loving only

OUR GENERATION HAS THE OPPORTUNITY TO MAKE LOVE A PUBLIC ETHIC ACROSS EVERY SECTOR OF OUR COMMON LIFE.

opponents is self-loathing, and loving only others is ineffective. Love must be practiced in all three directions to be revolutionary. Today our movement is rightly focused on solidarity with others, but if we are cruel to our opponents or to ourselves along the way, we will burn out. Worse, we will become what we are resisting.

Our generation has the opportunity to make love a public ethic across every sector of our common life. We have the wisdom and resources to model and practice the love ethic inside schools, homes, businesses, markets, media, courts, prisons, houses of worship, and halls of power. Ponder the questions below in your heart and in your community:

LOVING OTHERS: SEE NO STRANGER
When you look at faces on the street or screen, say in your mind: Sister, Brother, Son, Daughter, Uncle, etc. Assume everyone you see is a part of yourself that you do not yet know. What will you now wonder about

them? What new stories and histories will you hear? As you see others in the fire, where do your feet want to move?

LOVING OPPONENTS: TEND THE WOUND

Who is your opponent? What do you need in order to tend to the wounds they inflict on you? Can you sense rage and grief in your body without hating them? Most people inflict harm out of their own sense of threat, real or perceived. What would happen if your opponent no longer felt threatened? What is required to change the cultures and institutions that allow your opponent to hurt you? How does this insight change the way you fight?

LOVING OURSELVES: BREATHE AND PUSH

What is your labor in the world, in your family, and in the movement? Whom do you pour love into, and who pours love into you? Who is pushing and breathing with you? How do you breathe? Can you breathe the wellness you want in the world into your own body and home? When rage and despair are all around us, joy nourishes our spirits and strengthens our resolve to fight for what is good and beautiful. What do you need to protect joy every day?

My son has begun to talk. When he says he loves me, I ask, "Where do you feel that love in your body?"

He answers without hesitation: "In my feet!"

"And what does love feel like in your feet?"

"Feels like chocolate!"

The labor of love is painful, but it can also be sweet. We may not be able to protect our children from the fire, but if we show them how to walk the path of love, they will inherit joy in the struggle. So with love in my feet, I take your hand and march on.

anuary 21, 2017

ND WITH A

MATT

S HA

Washington, D.C.

NOW WHAT?

Chicago

YOU FELT HOW POWERFUL WOMEN ARE WHEN WE RISE UP. KEEP RISING.

IT'S TIME TO GET INVOLVED AND STAY INVOLVED. PLEDGE TO DEDICATE A MINIMUM OF ONE DAY A MONTH TO TAKING ACTION, THEN JOIN UP WITH ONE OR MORE OF THE ORGANIZATIONS ON THE FOLLOWING PAGES.

We've grouped the organizations that follow according to the eight Women's March Unity Principles. They can all use our support. While there are many groups doing great work, this list focuses primarily on organizations that are smaller, more grassroots, and founded and led by people of color. Look them up to educate yourself and others, get involved in their work by placing calls to your elected officials, attending a protest, or simply learning about an issue that doesn't directly affect you but that demands action. You could also donate money. We promise, they'll all be happy to hear from you.

CIVIL RIGHTS

BLACK LIVES MATTER NETWORK
blacklivesmatter.com
This chapter-based national network works to validate black lives. It was born out of the #BlackLivesMatter social media movement founded by Patrisse Cullors, Opal Tometi, and Alicia Garza after George Zimmerman, the man who killed unarmed teenager Trayvon Martin, was acquitted.

Get involved: Check out the website to find a local chapter or event near you. March at a local protest and use the site's resources to learn about ways to combat antiblack racism in your communities.

BLACK YOUTH PROJECT 100 (BYP100)
byp100.org
BYP100 is an activist member-based organization of black 18- to 35-year-olds dedicated to creating justice and freedom for all black people. The organization focuses on leadership development, direct action organizing, and education through a black queer feminist lens.

Get involved: Become a BYP100 member by attending an orientation. There are chapters in New York City; the Bay Area; Chicago; Washington, D.C.; New Orleans; Detroit; and Durham, North Carolina.

SHOWING UP FOR RACIAL JUSTICE (SURJ)
showingupforracialjustice.org
SURJ is a national organization of antiracist groups for white people who want to dismantle the systems of white supremacy.

Get involved: Find a local chapter near you in the database on SURJ's website. Volunteer for an antiracism event near you or host your own antiracism house party.

COUNCIL ON AMERICAN-ISLAMIC RELATIONS (CAIR)
cair.com
CAIR is a grassroots civil rights and advocacy group that promotes the understanding of Islam in America, encourages dialogue, protects civil liberties, and empowers Muslim Americans to build coalitions and promote justice and mutual understanding.

Get involved: Sign up for action alerts that will prompt you to contact lawmakers to encourage legislation protecting Muslim Americans. Report incidents of Islamophobia. Book a workshop or invite a speaker to a local event.

AMERICAN CIVIL LIBERTIES UNION (ACLU)
aclu.org
ACLU has been working to defend civil liberties in the United States for nearly a century. The organization files legal cases in matters of civil liberties and lobbies Congress and local governments to pass and protect policies that promote civil liberties.

Get involved: Find events in your area (or create one) to promote or protest civil liberty issues affecting your community. Sign a petition or reach out to your local lawmakers to tell them to take action.

WORKERS' RIGHTS

FIGHT FOR $15
fightfor15.org

The Fight for $15 began in New York City in 2012, when 200 fast-food workers went on strike to demand a $15-per-hour wage and union rights. Today it's a global movement of fast-food workers, home health aides, child care providers, teachers, airport workers, adjunct professors, retail employees, and underpaid workers everywhere. Fight for $15 has already won raises for 22 million people.

Get involved: Sign up for the mailing list and follow Fight for $15 on social media for updates and calls to action.

NATIONAL DOMESTIC WORKERS ALLIANCE (NDWA)
domesticworkers.org

The organization aims to improve working conditions for domestic workers by organizing domestic workers, immigrants, and women and their families, and changing how society values them and the work they do.

Get involved: Volunteer to support the organization, whether that's through legal or policy expertise or design, communications, or finance (or something else!). You can also help sign up domestic workers to grow NDWA's database and find resources on how to ethically employ domestic workers in your own home.

ASIAN PACIFIC AMERICAN LABOR ALLIANCE (APALA)
apalanet.org

APALA is the first and only national organization of Asian American and Pacific Islander workers and serves as the bridge between the broader labor movement and the AAPI community. APALA's mission is to defend and advocate for the civil and human rights of AAPIs, immigrants, and all people of color.

Get involved: Take the #NotYourModelMinority pledge or send a message to your mayor about the importance of defending and expanding sanctuary cities by visiting APALA's website.

A BETTER BALANCE (ABB)
abetterbalance.org

ABB works to help people care for their families without sacrificing economic security. The organization promotes legal strategies that encourage flexible workplace policies, advocates for paid family leave, and fights to end discrimination against caregivers.

Get involved: Use the tools on the website to help support or start a movement to pass paid family leave in your state.

SEX WORKERS OUTREACH PROJECT-USA (SWOP-USA)
new.swopusa.org

SWOP-USA is a national social justice network dedicated to the fundamental human rights of people involved in the sex trade and their communities, focusing on ending violence and stigma through education and advocacy.

Get involved: SWOP-USA has chapters in 20 states. Head to the website to find your local chapter and obtain educational resources about sex workers' rights.

ENDING VIOLENCE

THE GATHERING FOR JUSTICE
gatheringforjustice.org
Part of ending violence in our communities means effecting change in the criminal justice system. The Gathering for Justice works to end child incarceration and eliminate the racial inequities in the criminal justice system.

Get involved: Sign up for a volunteer training session, then help one of the organization's programs that provides training in nonviolence or leadership programs for incarcerated youths.

#CUT50
cut50.org
Cut50 is a bipartisan initiative to reduce the population of incarcerated individuals by 50 percent while making communities safer. The organization runs advocacy campaigns for criminal justice reform, educates the public about our current criminal justice system, and mobilizes organizers to push for change.

Get involved: Volunteer to get involved in one of Cut50's public education campaigns.

KNOW YOUR IX
knowyourix.org
Founded in 2013, Know Your IX is a survivor- and youth-led organization that aims to empower students to end sexual and dating violence.

Get involved: Sign up to receive Know Your IX updates on new legislation, actions at schools across the country, and ways to support organizing. If you'd like to share your opinion or experience, Know Your IX offers advice on publishing op-ed pieces. You do not need to be a student or a survivor to get involved.

LIFE CAMP
peaceisalifestyle.com
LIFE Camp is a violence intervention and prevention organization. Its pioneering model helps teenagers develop critical-thinking skills, self-empowerment, and personal accountability. In Queens, New York, LIFE Camp helped the community achieve a record 525 days with no shootings in an area plagued by violence.

Get involved: Support Peace Week every January, honoring Dr. Martin Luther King Jr.'s legacy by encouraging youths ages 16 to 25, parents, and business and community leaders to take one personal action toward making peace a lifestyle. Take the Peace Week pledge and share it with your school, coworkers, family, and friends.

GIRLS EDUCATIONAL & MENTORING SERVICES (GEMS)
gems-girls.org
GEMS serves girls and young women who have experienced commercial sexual exploitation and domestic trafficking. Founded in 1998, GEMS has helped hundreds of young women and girls to exit the commercial sex industry and to develop to their full potential.

Get involved: GEMS trains volunteers in its entirely survivor-written curriculum. Find or schedule a training, view a webinar, or book GEMS for a workshop or conference. You can also host a viewing party of the film *Very Young Girls* to educate viewers about commercial sexual exploitation and domestic trafficking of girls and young women in the United States.

NATIONAL INDIGENOUS WOMEN'S RESOURCE CENTER (NIWRC)
niwrc.org
NIWRC supports culturally grounded grassroots advocacy and provides national leadership in the effort to end gender-based violence in indigenous communities. The group develops educational materials and programs, provides technical assistance, and promotes the development of policies that build the capacity of indigenous communities.

Get involved: Visit the website to find fact sheets and digital resources, watch webinars, join the NIWRC email list, or subscribe to its magazine.

REPRODUCTIVE RIGHTS

NATIONAL LATINA INSTITUTE FOR REPRODUCTIVE HEALTH (NLIRH)

latinainstitute.org/en

NLIRH elevates Latina leaders and builds Latina power by advancing the fundamental human right to reproductive health, dignity, and justice for Latinas and their families in the United States.

Get involved: Sign up to receive a monthly newsletter and information about local action events that help educate and influence policy.

SISTERSONG WOMEN OF COLOR REPRODUCTIVE JUSTICE COLLECTIVE

sistersong.net

SisterSong strengthens and amplifies the voices of indigenous women and women of color to achieve reproductive justice. It advocates for access to abortion and against public-health disparities, poverty, incarceration, and more.

Get involved: Participate in a reproductive justice training program to learn about the SisterSong framework for reproductive justice and how to apply it to other work.

PLANNED PARENTHOOD

plannedparenthood.org

For more than a century, Planned Parenthood has provided high-quality, affordable reproductive and preventive health care across the country.

Get involved: Volunteer at a clinic (they need all different kinds of skills) or join Planned Parenthood Action Mobile Network.

NARAL PRO-CHOICE AMERICA

prochoiceamerica.org

NARAL Pro-Choice America is an organization of activists across the country supporting reproductive freedom by advocating for access to abortion care, birth control, paid parental leave, and protections from pregnancy discrimination through education and political action.

Get involved: Organize an action party in your community, attend an event, or sign up to make calls for its latest campaign.

LGBTQIA+ RIGHTS

LGBTQIA+ RIGHTS TRANSGENDER LAW CENTER

transgenderlawcenter.org

Transgender Law Center works to change law, policy, and attitudes so that all people can live safely, authentically, and free from discrimination regardless of their gender identity or expression.

Get involved: Check out the online Action Center for a state-by-state legislative tracker map to learn about how you can take action on any trans-specific legislation happening in your state, to sign petitions, and submit hate incident reports if you witness a transphobic hate crime.

NATIONAL LGBTQ TASK FORCE

thetaskforce.org

The Task Force is the oldest national LGBTQ advocacy group. Today it works to mobilize activists to make sure LGBTQ people can enjoy freedom, justice, and equality in every aspect of their lives, including housing, employment, health care, and basic human rights.

Get involved: Get informed with statistics and report sheets on the website and check out the Task Force Actions to sign petitions, send emails, and find more ways to advocate for action protecting the rights of LGBTQ people.

SOUTHERNERS ON NEW GROUND (SONG)

southernersonnewground.org

SONG is a queer liberation organization made up of people of color, immigrants, undocumented people, people with disabilities, as well as working-class and rural or small-town LGBTQ people in the South. The community is united to challenge oppression and bring liberation for all.

Get involved: Become a member of SONG, which welcomes members from all corners of the United States, regardless of sexual orientation. Sign up on the website to learn more about community organizing and campaigns.

DISABILITY RIGHTS

ADAPT
adapt.org
ADAPT is a national grassroots community that organizes disability rights activists to engage in nonviolent direct action, including civil disobedience, to assure the civil and human rights of people with disabilities to live in freedom.

Get involved: Sign up for the newsletter. Attend or organize a local training in the organizational techniques of ADAPT. Attend a national action event.

AMERICAN ASSOCIATION OF PEOPLE WITH DISABILITIES (AAPD)
aapd.com
AAPD improves the lives of people with disabilities by increasing their political and economic power. The organization advocates for them to live independently and to have access to education, technology, employment, housing, health care, and the ability to vote.

Get involved: Volunteer as a mentor or coordinator to organize a disability mentoring day in your area or at your company. Register to vote and help promote accessibility of voting technology and polling places. Use the Disability Equality Index to find out if your company's disability inclusion policies and practices are good enough.

HELPING EDUCATE TO ADVANCE THE RIGHTS OF THE DEAF (HEARD)
behearddc.org
HEARD is an all-volunteer nonprofit organization that promotes equal access to the legal system for individuals who are deaf and for other people with disabilities. HEARD focuses on correcting and preventing deaf wrongful convictions, ending deaf prisoner abuse, decreasing recidivism rates for deaf returned citizens, and increasing representation of the deaf in the justice, legal, and corrections professions. HEARD maintains the only national database of deaf, hard-of-hearing, and deaf-blind detainees and prisoners.

Get involved: HEARD relies exclusively on the assistance of volunteers and is always looking for attorneys, students, interpreters, and concerned citizens to assist in its efforts. You can also attend HEARD's public meetings; support its awareness campaign; visit or become pen pals with a deaf or deaf-blind prisoner; or donate stamps, envelopes, and old or new ASL dictionaries.

DISABILITY VISIBILITY PROJECT (DVP)
disabilityvisibilityproject.com
DVP is an online community dedicated to recording, amplifying, and sharing disability stories and culture. DVP supports and amplifies the work of other organizations focused on disabled people by using social media and partnering in various campaigns such as #CripTheVote.

Get involved: Record and submit your disability story using the StoryCorps app, by visiting a StoryCorps booth in select cities, or by submitting a blog post via the DVP website. You can also follow DVP on social media or sign up for blog updates on the website.

IMMIGRANT RIGHTS

UNITED WE DREAM
unitedwedream.org
This nonpartisan network is the nation's largest immigrant youth–led organization. Immigrant youths and allies advocate for the dignity and fair treatment of immigrant youths and their families regardless of their immigration status.

Get involved: Join a deportation defense program to help stop unjust deportations. Find an affiliate organization in your area and ask how you can support its work.

NATIONAL NETWORK FOR IMMIGRANT AND REFUGEE RIGHTS (NNIRR)
nnirr.org
The NNIRR brings together diverse immigrant communities with partners for social and economic justice to defend and expand the rights of all immigrants and refugees.

Get involved: Take part in one of the many campaigns and programs, from raising awareness about the militarized border to advocating for fair wages and benefits at companies like Walmart. Find educational resources and workshops to support local dialogue around immigration reform.

DEFINE AMERICAN
defineamerican.com
This nonprofit media and culture organization uses the power of storytelling to change the way immigrants, identity, and citizenship are discussed in entertainment, news media, and film.

Get involved: Join a college chapter of Define American, share your own immigration story, pledge to use accurate language about immigrants and immigration issues, and find documentary films and other educational resources to share with your community.

BLACK ALLIANCE FOR JUST IMMIGRATION (BAJI)
baji.org
BAJI focuses on educating and engaging African American and black immigrant communities to organize and advocate for racial, social, and economic justice.

Get involved: Donate to BAJI to support its work and find resources on its website to help you support black immigrant communities.

MIJENTE
mijente.net
Mijente is a political home for multiracial Latinx and Chicanx strategists, media makers, cultural workers, action takers, writers, base builders, and theorists. The organization makes digital tools in English and Spanish accessible to Latinx change makers so they can start or join a campaign.

Get involved: Start a petition or learn how to organize a campaign on its website. You can also donate to support the work or become a digital partner to create custom campaigns.

ENVIRONMENTAL JUSTICE

MOVEMENT GENERATION JUSTICE & EQUALITY PROJECT
movementgeneration.org
Movement Generation Justice & Ecology Project inspires and engages in transformative action toward the liberation and restoration of land, labor, and culture. The organization is committed to a just transition from profit and pollution to healthy, resilient, and life-affirming local economies.

Get involved: Movement Generation facilitates workshops and strategy sessions to develop a shared analysis of the ecological crisis and its impact on working-class communities and communities of color. Participate in a workshop, download curriculum materials, and donate to the organization on its website.

350
350.org
This global grassroots climate movement organizes public actions and online campaigns to oppose new coal, oil, and gas projects, and to take money from companies contributing to climate change in favor of clean energy solutions.

Get involved: Start a local group in your area. Join a campaign to stop the Keystone XL pipeline, help UNESCO cultural heritage sites kick out coal plants, and spread the word about the Paris Climate Agreement, or start your own climate petition using 350.org's online tools.

GREENPEACE
greenpeace.org/usa
Greenpeace uses peaceful protest and creative communication to expose global environmental problems and promote solutions for a green and peaceful future.

Get involved: Sign up for Greenpeace's email list and receive calls to action on its issues.

SIERRA CLUB
sierraclub.org
The Sierra Club is the nation's largest and most influential grassroots environmental organization, founded in 1892 by conservationist John Muir.

Get involved: Find a cause to support on the Programs and Campaigns section of the website. Look for the Grassroots Action Network to join volunteers making a difference on the environment where you are. The site also tracks the most urgent legislation to contact Congress about.

NATURAL RESOURCES DEFENSE COUNCIL (NRDC)
nrdc.org
The NRDC brings together environmental lawyers, scientists, businesses, elected leaders, community activists, and policy advocates to protect the earth's people, plants, and animals.

Get involved: Sign up for action alerts so you can reach out to your elected representatives to let them know how you feel about legislation affecting the climate. Learn ways to reduce your personal energy use. Using NRDC resources, start a community project to block the biggest polluters from setting up shop in your area.

Chicago

CAN'T PICK JUST ONE ISSUE?

If you want to think more intersectionally about how issues are interconnected, check out organizations that are taking on more than one issue at a time.

INDIVISIBLE was launched after the 2016 election to resist the agenda of the Trump administration. Each week you can check the website to find direct actions to take on the most pressing issues of the moment. Use the Indivisible Guide to start your own local grassroots movement to create change right where you are. **indivisible.org**

MOMSRISING is a national network of mothers and those who support them mobilizing grassroots actions that influence issues facing women, mothers, and families. Join a local group, sign a letter or petition, tell your own story of an issue you've faced, and sign up for the newsletter that shares opportunities to be involved. **momsrising.org**

MOVEON.ORG helps you take the first step toward grassroots change by signing and starting your own political petitions about issues you're passionate about. **moveon.org**

MPOWER CHANGE is a Muslim-led online organizing platform working to build the political power and capacity of Muslim communities and to lend Muslim voices to economic, social, and racial justice movements and campaigns. **mpowerchange.org**

PICO is a national network of faith-based community organizations working to create innovative solutions to problems facing all communities. Find a PICO group in your community and take action on urgent issues. **piconetwork.org**

THINKING EVEN BIGGER PICTURE? HOW ABOUT RUNNING FOR OFFICE?

If you've ever considered it, check out these organizations that can help you find out if politics is for you and help you get started.

EMERGE AMERICA recruits Democratic women who want to run for office and offers them an in-depth six-month, 70-hour training program. In the November 2016 election, 70 percent of its 214 alumnae won their elections. **emergeamerica.org**

EMILY'S LIST supports women candidates for national public office who are pro-choice and will make a significant contribution to education, health care, voting rights, and economic equality. You can start here to sign up for candidate training that will teach you what it really takes to run for office. **emilyslist.org**

HIGHER HEIGHTS is building a national infrastructure to harness black women's political power and leadership potential. Become a Higher Heights member and commit to building, expanding, and sustaining a national political infrastructure to strengthen black women's political power and leadership capacity. **higherheightsforamerica.org**

RUN FOR SOMETHING was started by two millennial political insiders seeking to support and train progressive millennials (and political outsiders) to run for office. Reach out if you're a millennial looking to run for office or are interested in helping to support the mission. **runforsomething.net**

SHE SHOULD RUN is a nonpartisan nonprofit that provides community, resources, and growth opportunities for aspiring political leaders. More than 15,000 women have been inspired to run for office through She Should Run since the 2016 election. **sheshouldrun.org**

Im in ♥ with
an IMMI GRANT.

Washington, D.C.

Las Vegas

BY CASSADY FENDLAY, SARAH SOPHIE FLICKER, AND PAOLA MENDOZA

AFTERWORD

At the end of the Women's March, we organizers turned to one another and said, "This is only the beginning."

Today this is no longer true. We have more than begun. A year has passed since the march, and we have continued to mobilize and organize in service to the Unity Principles of the Women's March.

Where we go from here depends on each one of us. Each of you holds an extraordinary amount of light. A light that people will follow. A light that will illuminate the path forward. Women are shepherding the resistance, from making calls to their representatives, to running for office on every level, to speaking to our kids about justice, to being dragged out of Congressional offices in wheelchairs in order to protect health care access. Indigenous women have chained themselves to heavy equipment owned by big oil corporations to protect our water. Through this leadership, we will birth a new nation, born of a new vision that looks far beyond the Trump administration.

In fact, in order to regain ground lost on equity and justice, we'll need engagement beyond resisting Trump. From the beginning, our collective has said that while he represents the most extremist and bigoted positions, we can't be lulled into the false sense that getting rid of him is going to be enough. He represents the problem, but he is not the problem alone. It is the groundwork that organizers lay, day after day, to dismantle the systems of oppression that enable moments like January 21 to spring to life.

To dismantle intersecting forms of oppression, we must remember this: that while women are a majority—we are over 50 percent of the population—we are not a monolith, and we will not always agree. Agreement on every issue is not the goal; in fact, that can be dangerous. But regardless of issue, our agreement must lie in the recognition, respect, and primacy of each person's basic humanity. This fundamental truth is at the heart of every spiritual tradition, and tolerating anything less is the greatest threat to our movement.

What we learned through organizing the Women's March is that if we aren't OK with being uncomfortable, we probably aren't doing it right. If we aren't tackling the issues that have historically held us back from truly being an inclusive movement, then we need to take a deep breath and dig deeper.

We came together holding fiercely to the wisdom of the giants who came before us, as well as with an eye on the mistakes made in the past. As Gloria Steinem says, if it's not intersectional, it's not feminism, and intersectional feminism inherently requires that we show up for all women. Not just sometimes. Not just when we agree.

What you've read here is as much of a blueprint as we can give you. The only way to keep learning is to go and do the work. The everyday work of organizing in your community. The internal work of understanding your privilege and how to use that privilege for communities that are not your own. The courageous work of having daring discussions, holding space for complexity and nuance, both with those whose opinions differ dramatically from yours and those whose opinions only slightly vary. White supremacy, patriarchy, and xenophobia are bedrocks of this country. However, in this lightless moment, we are presented with the luminous opportunity to reject these structures. The veil has been lifted. We have to love each other more than we love these institutions and systems. It is in the natural order of things that, as change rattles the cages of oppression, an inevitable pushback will occur. We must continue to rattle those cages and push back with equal force that is grounded in love, clarity, and intention.

Will you tire? Yes, of course you will. We have also been tired. Will you burn out because the injustice is too great? Because the patriarchy is too strong? Because the racism is too ingrained? Please do not—we cannot lose you. When you are at the precipice, about to turn back, dig into love. When you organize out of a place of love—love for your community, love for democracy, love for freedom—you cannot burn too bright. This type of love is infinite. In this love you will find the endurance to organize, to resist, to fight, and to envision a better world. Let love feed and inspire you. Love is your strongest tool against oppression.

The America we want to birth is possible, but it is not inevitable. Progress is not horizontal, nor is it continuous. We know that the status quo cannot be maintained without the acquiescence of the people. We must continue to show up intentionally and with strategy, and to do so even for those we do not know, with the commitment to the fundamental truth that *my liberation is bound in yours, and yours in mine*.

Chicago

Los Angeles

WE WILL FIGHT FOR CIVIL RIGHTS

WOMEN'S RIGHTS ARE HUMAN RIGHTS

WE'RE ON THE RIGHT SIDE OF HISTORY

#LOVE ARMY

Washington, D.C.

ACKNOWLEDGMENTS

Together We Rise, like the Women's March itself, was an extraordinary collaboration and we will be forever thankful for the help of the following individuals:

Cindi Leive, our champion and persister; you made this book happen with love and leadership. Jamia Wilson, your tireless work on our oral history wove our story into the fabric of American history. David Kuhn and Kate Mack, our agents at Aevitas Creative Management, moved this book from idea to accepted proposal with spectacular speed, while Quinn Heraty, our magnificent lawyer, was our superwoman! We are grateful to Erin Hobday, managing editor at Condé Nast, who shepherded this project from day one. To Dana Points, our project manager and editor on the book: Your guidance, passion, and commitment to excellence allowed this book to fly. Thanks to Chloe Scheffe, who designed the interior of the book, and to Paul Ritter, who masterminded its memorable cover. Kate Cunningham, our photography editor, dug into a trove of photographic treasures and pulled out the brightest gems. And a big thank-you goes to Jessica Sindler, our editor at Dey Street, whose sharp eyes reviewed every page at every stage. Our appreciation also goes to Virginia Heffernan and Maggie Mertens, reporters who contributed to the book, and to the team at Condé Nast who gave the manuscript and design their talent and time: Kimberly Bernhardt, Anastasia Casaliggi, Tess Kornfeld, Alanna Greco, Samantha Leach, Kevin Roff, and Patricia J. Singer. Jess McIntosh: You have been with us from the beginning. Thank you for reading these words when they were in their infancy. And, finally, we send our boundless thanks to all the photographers who contributed their work to this book. You'll find their names and details about which images they captured on pages 319 to 321.

Without a Women's March we would have no *Together We Rise*. So to all the march organizers across the country and the world, we thank you and are proud to stand shoulder to shoulder with you! The Women's March would not have been possible without your tireless dedication, your sleepless nights, and your belief in a more just and equitable world. Boundless gratitude goes to our national organizers and volunteers.

Jamiah Adams	Lauren Besser	Kate Catherall
Colleen Arnerich	David Bordow	Rebecca Abou-Chedid
Conrad Amenta	Sarah Boison	Ting Ting Cheng
Brea Baker	Jasmine Blackmon	Joy Cook
Kisha Bari	Helen Brosnan	Lisa Conn
LaMon Bland	Allyson Carpenter	Stefanie Cruz

ACKNOWLEDGMENTS

Peggy Dahlquist
Eisa Davis
Mike Dunn
Samantha Duberstein
Danielle DePalma
Esther de Rothschild
Rachel Ekroth
Diana Ezrins
Kelli Farr
Sam Frank
Tina Frank
Carmela French
Hayne Beattie Gray
Rachel Goldstein
Daria Hall
Tee Hanible
Evvie Harmon
Lisa Harps
Zach Helder
Nona Hendryx
Jackson Hyland-Lipski
Ganessa James
Avery Jones
Juliette Jones

Nalini Jones
Morley Shanti Kamen
Danielle Kwateng
Jenna Lautner
Stacey Lee
Dr. Tamara Lee
Eden Lewis
Carolyn Malachai
Joanie Michele
Stephanie Miliano
Allison Miller
Michelle Minguez
Stephanie Miliano
Melissa Mobley
Becky Morrison
Alex Nolan
Nicole Okumu
Kyle O'Leary
Jessi Olsen
Jasmine Partida
Nina Perez
Melody Rabe
Uma Ramiah
Sandra Restrepo

Genevieve Roth
ShiShi Rose
Hannah Rosenzweig
Ulysses Ruiz
Kim Parker Russell
Caitlin Ryan
Reshma Saujani
Karen Scott
Amanda Shepherd
Shabd Simon-Alexander
Heidi Solomon
Be Steadwell
Ianta Summers
Madison Thomas
Bridget Todd
Daveen Trentman
Tom Watson
Denise Willard
Brooke Williams
Tonya Williams
Joe Wilson
Oliver Hidalgo-Wohlleben

Our deepest gratitude also goes to the extraordinary visionaries who helped create the Unity Principles: J. Bob Alotta, Monifa Bandele, Zahra Billoo, Gaylynn Burroughs, Melanie L. Campbell, Sung Yeon Choimorrow, Alida Garcia, Alicia Garza, Indigenous Women Rise Collective, Carol Jenkins, Dr. Avis Jones-DeWeever, Carol Joyner, Janet Mock, Jessica Neuwirth, Terry O'Neill, Carmen Perez, Jody Rabhan, Kelley Robinson, Kristin Rowe-Finkbeiner, Linda Sarsour, Heidi L. Sieck, Emily Tisch Sussman, Jennifer Tucker and Winnie Wong. Your radical imagination is our guide during these tumultuous times.

And to the five million people who came out and marched on January 21, 2017: Keep showing up!

CREDITS

Cover photograph by Michael Skolink

Ash Adams, pp. 194–195

Brian Allen / Voice of America, p. 6

Christopher Anderson / Magnum Photos, p. 105

Alex Arbuckle, p. 183 bottom

Amy Arbus, p. 113

Nancy Bacher , p. 277

Ben Baker / Redux, p. 125

Kisha Bari, pp. 29, 32–33, 39, 43, 48, 77, 81, 94, 99, 100–101, 120–121, 129, 136–137, 167 top, 181 bottom, 183 top, 189, 238, 250, 252, 255, 256, 258–259, 262, 273 top, 281

Nina Berman / NOOR, p. 56

Cass Bird pp. 54-55, 197

Brian van der Brug/ *Los Angeles Times* via Getty images, p. 239

Kristian Buus / In Pictures via Getty Images, pp. 154-55

Jessica Chou, pp. 190–191

Mike Coppola / Getty Images, p. 176

Nicole Craine for *The New York Times*, pp. 210–211

Denise Crew / AUGUST, p. 90

Andy Cross / *The Denver Post* via Getty Images, pp. 220–221

Wiktor Dabkowski / ZUMA Press/Splash News, p. 222

Peter DaSilva, p. 266

Pari Dukovic, pp. 4, 219

Bryan Dumas, p. 270

Natan Dvir / Polaris/ Newscom, p. 142

Don Emmeret / Getty Images, p. 203 top

Elainea Emmott, p. 47

Jonathan Ernst / Reuters, pp. 172–173

Holly Falconer, p. 152

Eric Feferberg / AFP/ Getty Images, p. 144

Larry Fink, p. 285

Demetrius Freeman, p. 261

Ruth Fremson / *The New York Times* /Redux, p. 234

Noam Galai / WireImage/Getty Images, p. 82

Chelsea Guglielmino/ Getty Images, p. 132

Michelle Gustafson, p. 177 top

Leeta Harding, p. 246

Gabriela Hasbun, p. 126

Todd Heisler /

The New York Times / Redux, p. 26

Tony Herbas, pp. 22–23

Gabriela Herman, p. 200

Bryon Jaybee / Anadolu Agency/Getty Images, p. 151

Terrence Jennings, p. 316

Katherine Jones / Idaho Statesman/TNS via Getty Images, p. 196

Annalise Kaylor / ZUMA Press/Newscom, p. 68

Roger Kisby / Redux, p. 308

Dan Kitwood / Getty Images, p. 163

Erin Labelle / ImageBrief.com, p. 265

Adrees Latif / Reuters, p. 122

Zach Lewis, p. 278

Sara Naomi Lewkowicz, pp. 34, 228, 242, 289

Dina Litovsky / Redux, pp. 10, 44, 225

Steffi Loos / Getty Images, p. 153

Samantha Madar / Jackson Citizen Patriot via AP, p. 71

Amber Mahoney, pp. 62, 97, 110–111, 167 bottom, 187, 290, 307

Yael Malka, p. 131

Amanda Marsalis, p. 164

Paul Matzner / ImageBrief.com, p. 193

Kevin Mazur / Getty Images, p. 203 bottom

Emma McIntyre / Getty Images, p. 114

Susan Meiselas / Magnum Photos, p. 230 bottom

Brook Mitchell / Getty Images, p. 147

Sally Montana, pp. 64, 186, 207

Paul Morigi / Getty Images, pp. 160, 177 bottom

Sarah Morris / Getty Images, p. 72

Robert Nickelsberg / Getty Images, p. 138

Kevin O'Leary, p. 209

Keri Oberly, p. 108

Matthew Pillsbury, p. 24

Brian Powers / Gallery Stock, p. 204

David Ramos / Getty Images, p. 150

Dominick Reuter / Getty Images, pp. 168, 227

Jessica Rinaldi / *The Boston Globe* via Getty Images, p. 17

Jennifer Roberts for *The Globe and Mail*, pp. 21, 141

Abby Ross / Massif, pp. 118, 312–313

Greta Rybus, p. 20

Alyssa Schukar, pp. 78, 296, 305, 311

Matthew Septimus, p. 171

Dakota Sillyman / Getty Images, pp. 198–199

Aaron Smith / Gallery Stock, p. 67 top

Kelsey Stanton / BFA / REX / Shutterstock, p. 184

Victoria Stevens / AUGUST, p. 294

Doug Strickland / *Chattanooga Times Free Press* via AP, p. 179

Matt Stuart / Magnum Photos, pp. 232, 240

Ginny Suss, p. 273 bottom

Sara Swaty, p. 40

Mario Tama / Getty Images, pp. 18–19

Wayne Taylor / Getty Images, pp. 148–149

Pete Thompson / Gallery Stock, pp. 182, 230 top, 282

Sabrina Thompson, pp. 181 top, 192, 314–315

Jessica Torres, p. 50

Theo Wargo / Getty Images, p. 156

Michael S. Williamson / *The Washington Post* via Getty Images, p. 31

Kate Wool, p. 208

Marcus Yam / *Los Angeles Times* / Polaris, p. 36

Allison Zaucha, pp. 60, 102, 174–175, 212, 245

Linda Zunas, p. 67 bottom

Amplifier / p. 85, clockwise from top left: Brooke Fischer, Alexandria Lee, Mari Mansfield, Dawline-Jane Oni-Eseleh; p. 87, Jessica Sabogal; p. 88, clockwise from top left: Liza Donovan, Kafesha Thomas, Katie Rita, Kelley Wills

TIME photo illustration, Photograph by Danielle Amy Staif for *TIME*

TIME cover © 2017 Time Inc. Used with the permission of Time Inc., p. 237.

The March, by Abigail Gray Swartz, Cover of *The New Yorker*, Feb. 6, 2017, © 2017 *The New Yorker* & Abigail Gray Swartz

HarperCollins books may be purchased for educational, business, or sales promotional use. For information, please email the Special Markets Department at SPsales@harpercollins.com.

FIRST EDITION

Library of Congress Cataloging-in-Publication Data has been applied for.

ISBN 978-0-06-284343-2

18 19 20 21 22   QGT   10 9 8 7 6 5 4 3 2 1

2-5-18

Ingram

16.50

DISABILITY RIGHTS CIVIL RIGHTS REPRODUCTIVE RIGHTS RIGHTS WO ENDING V ENVIRONMENTAL JUSTICE LGBTQI IMMIGRANT RIG